DAILY
TEACHINGS

Rhonda Byrne

ATRIA BOOKS

NEW YORK   LONDON   TORONTO   SYDNEY   NEW DELHI

A Division of Simon & Schuster, Inc.
1230 Avenue of the Americas
New York, NY 10020

www.thesecret.tv

First Atria Books hardcover edition August 2013

ATRIA B O O K S and colophon are trademarks of Simon & Schuster, Inc.

For information about special discounts for bulk purchases, please contact Simon & Schuster Special Sales at 1-866-506-1949 or business@simonandschuster.com.

Book design by Gozer Media P/L (Australia), www.gozer.com.au, directed by The Secret.

Manufactured in the United States of America

10 9 8 7 6 5 4 3 2 1

ISBN: 978-1-4767-5193-1
ISBN: 978-1-4767-5194-8 (ebook)

"When you become aware of this great law, then you become aware of how incredibly powerful you are, to be able to THINK your life into existence."

Rhonda Byrne

The Secret

Dedicated to you

The Secret contains clear principles on how to live your life in accordance with the natural laws of the Universe, and the most important thing for any person to do is to LIVE IT. You can only become the master of your life by LIVING IT!

As we travel through a year of teachings, the clarity, understanding, and wisdom you will receive every day will help you live the laws that govern human beings, so you may truly become the master of your life.

May the joy be with you,

Rhonda Byrne

$\mathcal{T}$o change your life fast, use gratitude to shift your energy. When you put all of your energy into gratitude, you will see miracles take place in your life.

To change things quickly, commit to writing one hundred things you are grateful for each day, until you see the change. And FEEL the gratitude. Your power is in the FEELING that you put into the words of gratitude.

Whatever feelings you have within you are attracting your tomorrow.

Worry attracts more worry. Anxiety attracts more anxiety. Unhappiness attracts more unhappiness. Dissatisfaction attracts more dissatisfaction.

AND...

Joy attracts more joy. Happiness attracts more happiness. Peace attracts more peace. Gratitude attracts more gratitude. Kindness attracts more kindness. Love attracts more love.

Your job is an *inside* one. To change your world, all you have to do is change the way you feel inside. How easy is that?

$\mathcal{T}$he Universe is guiding you and communicating with you in every second of your life. It is responding to your thoughts and it is giving you invaluable feedback through your feelings. Your feelings are cosmic communication! The good feelings mean, GOOD FOR YOU. The bad feelings are to get your attention so that you will change what you are focusing on.

Tune in to the cosmic communication that is with you every day. You are never alone, not for a second. The Universe is right with you at every step, guiding you. But you have to listen!

*L*ook for the gifts in everything, especially when you are facing what appears to be a negative situation. Everything that we attract causes us to grow, which means that ultimately everything is for our own good.

Adjusting to a new path and a new direction will require new qualities and strengths, and these qualities are always exactly what we need to acquire in order to accomplish the great things ahead in our life.

No matter where you are, no matter how difficult things might appear to be, you are always being moved toward magnificence. Always.

"Happiness depends upon ourselves."

Aristotle (384–322 BC)

*T*here are two words that, when spoken, have the most unfathomable power to completely change your life. Two words that, when they pass your lips, will be the cause of bringing absolute joy and happiness to you. Two words that will create miracles in your life, wipe out negativity, and bring you abundance in all things. Two words that, when uttered and sincerely felt, will summon all the forces in the Universe to move all things for you.

There are just two words standing between you, happiness, and the life of your dreams...

THANK YOU.

*W*e attract to ourselves what we hold inside. Every circumstance, every person, and every situation that we attract and experience is based on what is inside of us. Could you ask for a more magnificent system than this?

Your life is a reflection of what you hold inside you, and what you hold inside you is always under your control.

*Y*ou are a unique and magnificent human being. Of all the billions of people on the planet, there is not another You, and your very existence is vital to the functioning of our Universe, because you are one part of the whole Universe. All that you see, and all that there is, could not exist without you!

$\mathcal{H}$ere is a simple, powerful process that you can do every day to bring yourself into positive harmony with the Universe and the law of attraction.

Sit down comfortably. Notice how you are feeling, and now relax your entire body. When you have relaxed your whole body, then relax it some more. Now relax it even more. And relax it more! Repeat this deeper relaxing seven times, each time relaxing as much as you can. When you have finished, notice the difference in how you are feeling, compared with how you felt when you began.

Now you are more in harmony with the Universe and the law of attraction!

$\mathcal{P}$ersist, persist, persist, and you will reach a point where the principles of The Secret become second nature to you. You will become so aware of the words that people speak, especially when they speak of things they don't want. You will become so aware of the words that *you* speak.

When you reach this point, it is a sign that you are becoming more and more aware! You are becoming more consciously aware!

$\mathcal{E}$ach of us is attracting in every moment of our lives. So when you feel that the law isn't working for you because you don't have what you want, realize that the law *is* responding to you. You are either attracting what you want or you are attracting the absence of what you want.

The law is still working.

"The greatest revolution in our generation is the discovery that human beings, by changing the inner attitudes of their minds, can change the outer aspects of their lives."

William James (1842–1910)

$\mathcal{B}$eginning to ask questions about life is a sign you are having a major breakthrough.

The Truth of Life is right here for everybody, as it has always been, but only the ones who ask questions receive the answers and discover the truth. When we ask questions, deeply wanting to know the answers, we will attract the answers in a form that we can understand.

To receive answers in life, you must begin to ask.

*L*ove is the highest power we possess to be in complete harmony with the law of attraction. The more love we feel, the greater our power. The more selfless love we feel, the more unfathomable our power.

The law of attraction has been called the law of love, because the law itself is a gift of love to humanity. It is the law by which we can create incredible lives for ourselves.

The more love we feel, the greater our power to create a magnificent life of love, joy, and harmony.

What does it feel like to be in harmony with the Universe?

It is the same feeling as when you float on water. If you are tense, or if you resist the water, you will sink. If you surrender to the water, the water will support you and you will float. That is the feeling, and that is how you harmonize yourself with the Universe.

Let the tension go and float!

*A*ccording to the law of attraction, the path to eradicating disease is not to fight it. If you decide you are going to fight a disease, your focus is on fighting the disease, and we attract what we are focusing on. Allow the doctors you have chosen to do their work, and keep your mind focused on well-being.

Think thoughts of well-being. Speak words of well-being. And imagine yourself completely well.

One of the biggest things you can do to change your circumstances around money is to take ten percent of what you receive and give it away. This is called the spiritual law of tithing, and it is the greatest action you can take to bring more money into your life.

*W*hy is it that most often you find that top-quality cars are kept immaculately clean and tidy by their owners, while the older cars are often dirty and messy inside?

The difference is the evidence of appreciation.

Appreciation of what you have brings what you want.

That is how those people attracted the better cars to them.

"Never try to compel others to change; leave them free to change naturally and orderly because they want to; and they will want to when they find that your change was worthwhile.

"To inspire in others a desire to change for the better is truly noble; but this you can do only by leaving them alone, and becoming more noble yourself."

Christian D. Larson (1874–1954)

Mastery of Self

*G*ood is underneath every single thing that appears to be negative. If we can know that good is all there is, including in a negative situation, then we will see a negative situation transform into all good. Most people keep the good away from themselves because they label something as bad, and then, of course, that becomes their reality. But there is no bad in the Universe; it is just our inability to see things clearly from the bigger perspective.

Peace comes from knowing that good is all that exists.

*Y*ou are in a partnership with the law of attraction, and it is through this partnership between the two of you that you are creating your life. Each person has their own personal partnership with the law of attraction. You use the law for yourself; everyone else uses the law for themselves. You cannot use the law of attraction on someone else, *against their free will*. And when you think about it, thank goodness the law operates this way. If it did not, then anybody else could create something in your life that you did not want.

You create through your thoughts and feelings, and no one but you can think your thoughts or feel your feelings.

*I*f you have a friend who is going through any kind of difficult time, help them by making sure you maintain *your* joy. Your good feelings will help lift them. You can also help them by directing their conversations so that they speak about what they want. As they fall into speaking about what they don't want, just keep gently leading them back to speaking about what they want. You can also speak to them as though their difficult time is over, and suggest they imagine that it has all passed and worked out beautifully.

Be the conductor when you speak with them, and help them stay in tune with the Universe.

$\mathcal{Y}$ou can change the path of your life from dark to light or from negative to positive. Every single time you focus on the positive you are bringing more light into your life, and you know that light removes all darkness. Gratitude, love, kind thoughts, words, and actions bring light and eliminate the darkness.

Fill your life with the light of positivity!

When you are just beginning to deliberately manage the frequency of your being (through your thoughts and feelings), you may find there are some ups and downs, and that you are jumping from one frequency to another. This stage is so short, and in no time at all you will begin to stabilize on a higher frequency, and then a higher frequency, forever climbing higher and higher.

It took some practice to walk, didn't it? But with determination you did it. There is no difference.

"A feeling that greater possessions, no matter of what kind they may be, will *of themselves* bring contentment or happiness, is a misunderstanding. No person, place, or thing can give you happiness. They may give you cause for happiness and a feeling of contentment, but the Joy of Living comes from within."

Geneviève Behrend (1881–1960)

Your Invisible Power

$\mathcal{T}$o create your tomorrow, go over your day tonight when you are in bed just before you fall asleep, and feel gratitude for the good moments. If there was something you wanted to happen differently, replay it in your mind the way you wanted it to go. As you fall asleep, say, "I will sleep deeply and wake up full of energy. Tomorrow is going to be the most beautiful day of my life."

Good night!

When it comes to love relationships, often people think that they want a particular person. But if you think about it deeply, it is not really the particular person that they want. What they really want is to be blissfully happy with the *perfect* person. Yet still they try and tell the Universe WHO that person is. If the Universe isn't delivering, then the message from the Universe is loud and clear: "I just checked twenty years ahead, and the bliss and happiness you deserve will not happen in this relationship."

Why is it that we think we know more than the one who can see everything?

$\mathcal{P}$lanet Earth and humanity need you. They need you, and that is why you are here.

$\mathcal{Y}$ou have the ability to command anything. Here is something you can say to command that negative thoughts leave you:

"Be gone! You have no part in me. I am Spirit. I harbor only the good and perfect thoughts of Spirit."

Never were truer words spoken.

*F*rom the moment you are born, you have a cosmic partner who never leaves your side throughout your whole life. This cosmic partner has unbelievable contacts, and unlimited means and ways of doing anything you want. Time is no obstacle, size is no problem, and space doesn't exist for your cosmic partner. There isn't anything your partner cannot do for you.

And all you have to do is follow the cosmic rules. Ask, and then really believe that in the moment you ask, what you desire is already yours.

Imagine it – the entire Cosmic Universe batting for you!

$\mathcal{D}$id you know that if your life was not changing, you would not exist? Our Universe and everything in it is continually changing, because our Universe is made of energy. Energy can exist only if it is in motion and changing. If energy stopped being in motion, our entire Universe and all Life would vanish.

Our lives are also energy, and therefore they too must always be in motion and continue to change. You cannot stop the motion and change in your life, nor would you want to. The changing nature of energy gives us Life. It causes Life to grow and causes us to grow.

$\mathcal{T}$hink good thoughts.

Speak good words.

Take good actions.

Three steps that will bring more to you than you can ever imagine.

"The thought manifests as the word. The word manifests as the deed. The deed develops into habit. And the habit hardens into character. So watch the thought and its ways with care. And let it spring from love, born out of concern for all beings."

Buddha (c. 563–c. 483 BC)

The law of attraction is impersonal. It operates just like a photocopying machine. The law is photocopying what you are thinking and feeling in every moment, and then sending an exact photocopy back to you – which becomes your life. That makes your ability to change your entire world so very easy.

To change the outside world all you have to do is change the way you think and feel, and the law of attraction will photocopy the change.

To change our lives, at some point we have to decide that, rather than suffer anymore, we are going to live in happiness. And the only way we can do that is to make the decision to look for things to appreciate, no matter what.

As we begin to focus on the good and the brighter side of things, the law of attraction responds by sending back to us the exact photocopy of our new thoughts. And good things begin to appear. And then more good things, and then more...

We are all entirely free to choose whatever we want. The power is in your hands now, and you are the one who chooses how to use that power in your own life. You can choose:

To have a happier life today, or put it off until tomorrow.

What feels better? You choose.

*I*t is so important that you are grateful for everything in
your life. Many people focus on the one thing they want
and then forget to be grateful for all the things they have.
Without gratitude you cannot achieve anything through the
law of attraction, because if you are not emanating gratitude
from your being, then by default you are emanating
ungratefulness. Be proactive and use the frequency of your
being to receive what you want.

vision board is a tool to help you create the image in your mind of what you want. As you look at the vision board, you are imprinting the picture of your desire in your mind. As you focus on your vision board, it stimulates your senses and evokes a positive feeling within you. Then you have the two elements of creation – your mind and your feelings – working in full force.

$\mathcal{E}$instein told us that time is just an illusion. When you understand and accept that there is no time, you can see that whatever you want in the future already exists. That is why when you write, imagine, or speak of your desire, you should use the present tense. Radiate your desire in your mind, heart, and body, and see it as here *now*.

"No one is more cherished in this world than someone who lightens the burden of another."

Anonymous

---

*Y*ou have been using The Secret all of your life – there is no time when you haven't been using it. You are using it whether you bring things you want or things you don't want. Every person, event, and circumstance – in every single day – comes to you through the law of attraction.

$\mathcal{T}$he key to visualization is to keep the picture moving in your mind, and yourself moving in the picture. If you keep the picture moving like a movie, you can master visualization really quickly. If the picture is static, it is a lot harder to hold the picture in your mind.

Keep your visualization busy with lots of movement, and your mind will become so captivated it will not be able to think of anything else.

When you are beginning to create intentionally, it is often better to focus on one thing at a time. With practice you will have great power to harness your energy, and then you will be able to focus on many things at the one time.

Imagine your mind as a magnifying glass with the sun shining through it. As you hold the magnifying glass steady in one place, you will create a fire. There is no difference between a magnifying glass and the sun, and your mind and the Universe.

*I*f you are just beginning to use the principles of The Secret, my advice to you is to focus on working on the frequency of your being first. Ask for what you want, and then WORK on the inside of you. WORK on lifting the frequency of your being through your thoughts and feelings.

Tune your frequency to be in harmony with the Universe. The frequency of the Universe is a frequency of pure goodness!

$\mathcal{I}$f you want to attract more money, make lists of the things you will buy with the money. Surround yourself with pictures of the things you would like and always feel the feelings of having those things now. Imagine sharing those things with the ones you love and imagine their happiness.

Now you're creating!

There is no force of hate. Hate is simply the absence of love, just as darkness is the absence of light. Poverty is the absence of abundance, sickness is the absence of health, and sadness is the absence of joy. All negativity is simply the *absence* of something positive.

This is very, very good to know.

"The aim of life is self-development. To realize one's nature perfectly – that is what each of us is here for."

Oscar Wilde (1854–1900)

The Picture of Dorian Gray

$\mathcal{T}$ake a moment to think about all that nature gives to you every single day so that you can live. And yet nature never asks for anything in return.

That is true giving.

There is no doubt that when using the law of attraction for the good of everyone, you are connecting yourself to great power. However, the law is also available to you individually so that you may live your life to the fullest. When you live your life to the fullest you have so much more to give others.

Your pain and misery does not help the world. But your joy and your life lived fully uplifts the world.

$\mathcal{I}$f you are visualizing all of the time and nothing is happening, it means that you are overriding your intention in some other powerful way that you are not aware of. What are you thinking? What words are you speaking? What actions are you taking? If you're not sure, ask the law of attraction to show you where you are overriding your intention, and it will be shown to you clearly.

If you want to attract appreciation for what you do, then move through your life appreciating and complimenting others.

If you find fault with another, then you just brought others finding fault with you. If you judge another, then you just brought judgment to you. And if you appreciate others, you will bring appreciation to you. You have to make the quality dominant in you first, before you can attract it in your outside world.

$\mathcal{T}$he entire world and every single detail in your day are all showing you the frequency within you. The evidence of your frequency is speaking to you in every moment through the people that you experience, the circumstances, and the events.

Life is mirroring back to you what you are holding inside you.

*A*nybody who thinks negative thoughts about someone else has those negative thoughts return to them multiplied. It doesn't matter how many people are thinking negatively about someone; if that person is in joy those thoughts can never reach them, because they are on a different frequency. Instead, all the negative thoughts will multiply and return to the people who were thinking them.

No one else can bring negativity into our lives through their thoughts, unless we allow our frequency to lower to the same negative frequency as theirs.

"We are sending out thoughts of greater or less intensity all the time, and we are reaping the results of such thoughts. Not only do our thought-waves influence ourselves and others, but they have a drawing power – they attract to us the thoughts of others, things, circumstances, people, 'luck,' in accord with the character of the thought uppermost in our minds."

William Walker Atkinson

(1862–1932)
Thought Vibration

*T*o experience deep gratitude, sit down and write a list of the things you are grateful for. Keep writing your list until your eyes are overflowing with tears. As the tears come, you will feel the most beautiful feeling around your heart and all through the inside of you. This is the feeling of true gratitude. Once you have felt this feeling you will know how to re-create it.

This intense feeling of gratitude is the feeling you want to reproduce as many times a day as you can. In a very short time you will be able to bring that feeling into your body at any time, virtually instantaneously.

Practice will get you there.

*A*sk, Believe, Receive – just three simple steps to create what you want. However, very often the second step, *believe*, can be the most difficult one. And yet it is the greatest step you will ever take. *Believing* contains no doubt. *Believing* does not waver. *Believing* is absolute faith. *Believing* remains steadfast despite what is happening in the outside world.

When you master *believing*, you have mastered your life.

$\mathcal{D}$o you know that as you try and work out "how" your desire will come about, you are actually pushing your desire away from you? As you try and work out "how" you can make your desire happen, you are sending a huge message to the Universe that you do not have your desire. And if you're not emanating the exact frequency of having your desire from within you, how can the Universe possibly find your signal to deliver your desire?

*Y*ou are a transmission center of the Universe. You are emitting a frequency to the Universe every second and you are receiving transmissions back every second. To create what you want, you must telegraph your desire without breaking the transmission, and you do that by holding within you the knowledge that your desire has manifested.

But if you begin to have thoughts that your desire is not here, and if you begin to doubt, you just broke the transmission. The Universe has lost your signal and instead has received your new signal that you do not have your desire. The Universe responds unfailingly to your new signal, and you receive what you are transmitting: my desire is not here!

All you have to do is shift yourself back on to the frequency of *having* what you want, and the Universe can deliver it to you.

$\mathcal{T}$he Universe has unlimited ways to bring your dream about, and I can assure you that when you emanate your dream on the inside of you, it will appear in the outside world in a way that you could never have imagined.

Just get your emanation happening and leave the rest to the Universe.

*H*ow did I use The Secret to stop wearing reading glasses?

I asked, and then I visualized myself without reading glasses in every situation. My eyesight became clear in three days. I didn't notice the three days that it took because I KNEW it was done in the moment I asked. If I had noticed the three days that it took, then I would have been noticing that it was not already done. I totally believed and KNEW it was done. I had absolute faith. I can just as easily say that it took me three days to realize that my eyes were seeing clearly or that it took me three days to adjust to my clear eyes. That would be true, because I knew the moment I asked that it had been given to me, and I had absolutely no doubt whatsoever. From that state of knowing, my eyesight became clear in three days.

"If we live good lives, the times are also good. As we are, such are the times."

Saint Augustine Of Hippo (354–430)

*W*e can never bring anything to us unless we are grateful for what we have. In fact, if somebody was completely and utterly grateful for everything, they would never have to ask for anything, because it would be given to them before they even asked.

That is the power of Gratitude.

*A*ll you have to do is ask and believe, and then get yourself on the receiving frequency of goodness. You don't actually have to do anything else. The Universe will do all the moving of things, including moving you.

When you ask and believe, you are getting yourself out of the way so the Universe can do its work.

𝒟o not worry at all about negative thoughts, and do not try to control them. All you have to do is begin to think good thoughts each day. Plant as many good thoughts as you can in each day. As you begin to think good thoughts you will attract more and more good thoughts, and eventually the good thoughts will wipe out the negative thoughts altogether.

$\mathcal{T}$o allow the Universe to move you in your life to happier and better things, you are going to need to look around you and appreciate the good things here and now. Seek the beautiful things and count the blessings of where you are. Dissatisfaction will not bring the happier and the better into your life. Dissatisfaction roots you to the spot where you currently are, but appreciation for what you have attracts the happier and better to you.

Remember that you are a magnet! Appreciation attracts appreciation!

*W*hen there is a big change of energy that affects our lives, we often label it as "bad" and cause ourselves sorrow, pain, and suffering by resisting that change. But you always have a choice.

In the Universe there is never just one way, and you are never trapped with no way out, no matter what has occurred. In every circumstance and moment of your life there are two paths available to you. The two paths are the positive and the negative, and YOU are the one who chooses which path you will take.

When you ask for happiness and a beautiful life, ask not just for you, but for everyone. When you ask for something better, ask not just for you, but for everyone. By all means ask for abundance and health for you, but also ask for it to be given to everyone.

Can you imagine what would happen if six billion people asked for these things for you?

"If a man's mind becomes pure, his surroundings will also become pure."

Buddha (c. 563–c. 483 BC)

$\mathcal{T}$o understand how you might be thinking thoughts without realizing it, stop right now, close your eyes, and do not think a single thought for ten seconds.

If thoughts came even though you decided to stop them, you know thoughts are happening in your life without your knowledge of them. If your mind will not obey you and stop for ten seconds, can you imagine the amount of thoughts that are being produced in one day?

You can change this and master your mind. All it takes is practicing the process of not thinking a thought for ten seconds. In a short amount of time you will be able to stop all thoughts for ten seconds, fifteen seconds, thirty seconds, and so on, until *you* are the one who decides whether you will think a thought or not. The peace that comes when you are the master of your mind is indescribable, and along with that you will also be a master of the law of attraction. Imagine that!

*I*f you have "needing money" in your vibration, then you will keep attracting needing money. You have to find a way of being happy NOW, feeling good NOW, and being in joy NOW, without the money, because those great feelings are how you will feel *with* the money.

Money doesn't bring happiness – but happiness brings money.

$\mathscr{I}$f you had had a perfect existence up until now, where everything had gone exactly right, you might not have a strong determination and desire to change your life. It's all of the apparently "negative" things that happen to us which give us a huge desire to change things. That huge desire that arises within you is like a magnetic fire, and it is very powerful.

Be grateful for everything that caused that fire to ignite a massive desire within you, because that fire of desire will give you strength and determination, and *you will change your life.*

*A*ny words you speak have a frequency, and the moment you speak them they are released into the Universe. The law of attraction responds to all frequencies, and so it is also responding to the words that you speak. When you use very strong words, such as "terrible," "shocking," and "horrible" to describe any situation in your life, you are sending out an equally strong frequency, and the law of attraction must respond by bringing that frequency back to you.

The law is impersonal, and simply matches your frequency. Do you see how important it is for you to speak strongly about what you *want*, and not to use strong words about what you *don't* want?

$\mathcal{G}$et into the feeling of having what you want now, and keep feeling that. It will be the most wonderful feeling in the world. As you practice the feeling, it will get stronger and stronger. You will begin to feel that you already have what you want. When you do this, the law must respond.

Remember that the law has never failed in anything it has undertaken, and it will not fail in your case either.

When you were a small child playing make-believe, do you remember how convincing your imagination was to you? Well, this is what you must do when you want anything. Secretly, inside yourself, pretend that you have what you want already. For example, if you want friends, make believe or pretend that you have great friends now.

The moment you tip the balance by imagining and feeling that you have great friends now *more* than noticing that you don't, you will have great friends.

This simple formula applies to everything.

"Man is what he believes."

Anton Chekhov (1860–1904)

The Notebook of Anton Chekhov

*Y*our advancement in mastering the law of attraction is based on learning and then practicing what works best for you.

Every day you can see what you have been thinking through what is happening in your life. Your entire world is a movie, showing you how you are going. You are not in the dark – you are getting feedback. Learn from the feedback. Observe what comes to you easily and think about what you did for that thing to come easily.

Know yourself, and you will become a master of the law of attraction.

*O*ur natural state of being is joy. It takes so much energy to think negative thoughts, to speak negative words, and to feel miserable. The easy path is good thoughts, good words, and good deeds.

Take the easy path.

*A*ncient wisdom dating back thousands of years gave us the truth about gratitude. Every single religion speaks of giving thanks. All the sages and saviors of the world demonstrated the use of gratitude in all their teachings. The greatest human beings who have ever lived showed us the way with gratitude, and by their example became shining lights in our history.

Surely this is why Einstein said "Thank you" hundreds of times every single day!

$\mathcal{T}$he law of attraction is like a giant photocopying machine, giving back to you exactly what you are thinking and feeling. If things are coming into your life that you do not want, then it is certain that most of the time you are not aware of the thoughts you are thinking, or of your feelings. Become *aware* of your feelings so when you are not feeling good you can stop and change the way you feel. And how do you do that? You think thoughts that make you feel good.

Remember that you cannot think good thoughts and feel bad, because your feelings are the result of your thoughts.

The effective use of affirmations depends entirely on how much you believe them when you say them. If there is no belief, then the affirmation is just words that have no power. Belief adds power to your words.

When you believe what you say, you just created it, no matter what it is.

"In every word you use, there is a power germ which expands and projects itself in the direction your word indicates, and ultimately develops into physical expression. For example, you wish the consciousness of joy. Repeat the word 'joy' secretly, persistently, and emphatically. The repetition of the word 'joy' sets up a quality of vibration which causes the joy germ to begin to expand and project itself until your whole being is filled with joy. This is not a mere fancy, but a truth."

Geneviève Behrend (1881–1960)

Your Invisible Power

Whenever you remember, at any time of the day, say "I AM JOY." Say it hundreds of times a day if you like. Say it often, but say it very, very slowly, giving equal emphasis to each word. I – AM – JOY. Feel the meaning of the words as you slowly say them, and experience as much of a feeling of joy within you as you can. Build on that feeling every single day. You will get better and better at it.

Feel that joy inside you more than you react to outside circumstances, and you will change the outside circumstances.

Joy attracts joy.

*W*rite down all the great things about everyone you know. Make a huge list of all the wonderful things about you. Compliment people wherever you go. Praise every single thing you see. Be a ray of sunshine to everyone you meet, and make their day better for having seen you. Say "Thank you" at every turn. Walk, talk, think, and breathe appreciation and gratitude.

When you do this, your outer life will change to reflect your inner state of being.

$\mathcal{T}$he law of attraction is infallible, and every single person is getting what they are asking for, even though most of the time each person is not aware that they are asking for what they *don't* want. There is such absolute beauty in the law, which is so responsive and giving in every single moment so that we can experience our lives.

The law never changes – we must learn how to live in harmony with the law. That is the greatest task for every single human being.

$\mathcal{Y}$ou can turn your life into paradise, but the only way you can do it is to make the inside of you a paradise. There is no other way.

You are the cause; your life is the effect.

*W*hen you focus with someone on a problem they are having, you are not helping them *or* you, because you are both adding energy to the problem. You are also both attracting more "like" problems to you.

Knowing this, it's very important for you and the other person to focus on what you both want. The person with the problem should be encouraged to speak about what they want instead of about the problem, which is what they don't want. The problem arose in the first place from the person thinking or talking about what they didn't want, so the chain reaction must stop. Help those close to you by encouraging them to speak the words of what they want. That is always the solution.

Negative thoughts are not who you are. Your true nature is all good. So if by chance a negative thought comes, say to yourself, "These thoughts are not mine, and they do not belong with me. I am all good and I have only good thoughts for myself and everyone."

Now you are speaking the truth!

$\mathcal{H}$ere is a way to stop negative thoughts: Focus your mind on your heart. Breathe in deeply, keeping your focus on your heart. Really concentrate on feeling love in your heart. Breathe out holding your focus on your heart and feeling the love in your heart. Repeat this a total of seven times.

When you do this correctly, you will feel a very big difference in your mind and your whole body. You will feel more peaceful, you will feel lighter, and you will have stopped those negative thoughts.

"Except our own thoughts, there is nothing absolutely in our power."

René Descartes (1596–1650)

It is important to remember that it is your thoughts and feelings together that create with the law of attraction, and you cannot separate them. Also remember that it's your feelings that are summing up your overall frequency and telling you what you are creating in this moment.

So how are you feeling right now? Could you feel better? Well then, do what it takes right now to feel better.

$\mathcal{U}$se the power of the Universe by intending before every car trip that the traffic will flow effortlessly, that you will be relaxed and happy, and that you will arrive in perfect time.

Happy driving!

*I*ncorporating the rule of fair exchange in your life is living the law of attraction.

Be sure that you always give fair exchange in business and in your personal life. In business, always give more value than the money you receive. In your personal life, always give back what you have received. If you have received support from others at a time when you needed it, and then someone asks for your support, be sure to give back the support you have received. All support comes to you through the Universe, and so when you give support back you are giving back to the Universe.

This is living according to the rule of fair exchange, and it is living the law of attraction.

*Y*our life is in your hands, but you must learn to gain control of your thoughts. All of your problems of fear, failure, and doubts are because your MIND is ruling you. Your mind has taken over, and you are the slave and victim of your uncontrolled negative thoughts. It is as simple as that. Take control of your mind and your thoughts. Every day, bit by bit, watch your thoughts.

When a negative thought comes, stamp it out, and refuse to allow a negative thought to take root in you by thinking of something good instead. Think more and more and more good thoughts, and soon they will come automatically.

To still your mind, sit down each day, close your eyes, and just watch your thoughts. Don't resist the thoughts, but just watch them come into your mind. As you watch each thought, it will disappear. Practice this each day and you will get better and better. You will find your mind will be without thoughts for five seconds, and then ten seconds, and then twenty seconds.

When you can command your mind to be still and have it obey your command, just imagine the power you will have to create what you want.

*A*lways remember that your feelings are monitoring your thoughts *for* you. Your feelings are telling you whether you are thinking thoughts that are good for you or thoughts that are not good for you. If you can become more and more conscious of how you are feeling, then you will become more and more aware of what kind of thoughts you are thinking. Your feelings are unceasingly telegraphing messages to you.

Listen to your own being!

"Everything has its origin in the mind, and that which you seek outwardly, you already possess. No one can think a thought in the future. Your thought of a thing constitutes its origin."

Geneviève Behrend (1881–1960)

Your Invisible Power

*Y*ou are never alone in anything you do, unless you think you are alone, which is a scary thought for anyone. When you know that you have the power of the Universe responding to your every thought, waiting and ready to help you accomplish anything, then your fear will disappear.

You have the greatest ally, which has access to all energy everywhere. Nothing can stand in its way – and all you have to do for your Universal partner is believe.

$\mathcal{O}$ur natural state is joy, and you know that, because when you are in the opposite state you feel bad. So if joy is what you truly are, can you see that it takes much more energy for you to generate negativity than it does to be naturally joyful?

*A*nother easy way to use the law of attraction for your benefit is this:

Every night before you fall asleep, replay in your mind the good moments of the day, and give heartfelt thanks for each one of them. Think about the next day also, and intend that it is going to be amazing, that it is going to be filled with love and joy, and that all good is coming to you. Intend that it is going to be the best day of your life. Then when you wake in the morning, BEFORE you get out of bed, declare your intentions again for the day and give deep thanks as though you have received them all.

$\mathcal{T}$he word "if" has a powerful frequency of doubt. When you are thinking or speaking about what you want, discard the word "if" from your vocabulary. Can you see when you use the word "if" that you don't believe what you want is yours?

The law of attraction cannot give you what you want when you emanate doubt with the word "if." Only use the word "when" as you think or speak of what you want; "When this happens," "When I do this," "When I am there," "When this comes," "When I have that." WHEN, WHEN, WHEN!

Whether you know it or not, today you are placing an order for your tomorrows from the catalogue of the Universe. Your predominant thoughts and feelings today are creating a frequency that is automatically determining your life tomorrow.

Feel good now and for the rest of the day, and make your tomorrows magnificent.

*Y*ou must be happy now to bring happiness into your life through the law of attraction. It's a simple formula. Happiness attracts happiness. Yet people use so many excuses as to why they can't be happy. They use excuses of debt, excuses of health, excuses of relationships, and excuses of all sorts of things as to why they can't use this simple formula. But the formula is the law.

No matter what the excuse, unless you begin to feel happy despite it, you cannot attract happiness. The law of attraction is saying to you, "Be happy now, and as long as you keep doing that, I will give you unlimited happiness."

"A human being is a part of the whole, called by us 'Universe,' a part limited in time and space. He experiences himself, his thoughts and feelings as something separated from the rest – a kind of optical delusion of his consciousness. This delusion is a kind of prison for us, restricting us to our personal desires and to affection for a few persons nearest to us. Our task must be to free ourselves from this prison by widening our circle of compassion to embrace all living creatures and the whole of nature in its beauty. Nobody is able to achieve this completely, but the striving for such achievement is in itself a part of the liberation and a foundation for inner security."

Albert Einstein (1879–1955)

In the 1900s, Émile Coué (a French psychologist and pharmacist) was a pioneer in the work of using positive thoughts to aid in healing. Part of his successful healing methods involved the simple daily application by his patients of this conscious autosuggestion: "Every day, in every way, I am getting better and better." This is not only a powerful statement for health. As you can see by the words, it is a powerful statement for all areas of our life.

When using this affirmation, say it very slowly and with the full conviction of the meaning of the words. It is the force we put into words that makes them powerful.

*I*magine writing an email of what you want to the Universe. When you are happy that your email is very clear, you hit "Send" and you know your request has gone into the ethers. You also know that the Server of the Universe is an automatic system, and it doesn't question email requests. Its job is simply to fulfil every request.

If you begin to worry and stress that you haven't got what you wanted, then you have just sent another email to the Universe to stop your order. And then you wonder why you haven't received what you asked for.

Once you Ask, know that the Server of the Universe is an automatic infallible system that never fails, and expect to receive your request!

*H*ere is something you can do that is the one of the most powerful uses of the law of attraction. This exercise is thirty days of an avalanche of giving.

Every day for thirty consecutive days, give. Give joy, smiles, warm words, love, appreciation, and compliments to everyone you meet, including strangers, friends, and family. Speak from your heart, giving the very best of you in every moment of your day, and make it your mission to make every single person's day better with kind thoughts and words.

As you give the best of you, you will be staggered by the speed that it comes back to you.

*O*nce you know the law of attraction, you can make the best discoveries about yourself by listening to what you are saying.

When you state something as an absolute fact, realize that it is something you really believe, and that belief is creating it in your life. As you hear your words and realize that you are saying something you do not want, switch immediately and rephrase your sentence with the words of what you want. You will learn so much about your past experiences and what you have created when you listen to your words. And then, as you catch your words and change them, you are changing the entire course of your future!

The negative feeling of disappointment keeps your desire from you. To turn disappointment into a positive feeling, start thinking and saying, "WHEN my desire arrives I am going to..." And fill in the blank.

This is a great way to shift yourself to believing, and believing is where you want to be.

I promise myself...

To be so strong that nothing can disturb my peace of mind.

To talk health, happiness, and prosperity to every person I meet.

To make all my friends feel that there is something worthwhile in them.

To look at the sunny side of everything and make my optimism come true.

To think only of the best, to work only for the best, and to expect only the best.

To be just as enthusiastic about the success of others as I am about my own.

To forget the mistakes of the past and press on to the greater achievements of the future.

To wear a cheerful expression at all times and give a smile to every living creature I meet.

To give so much time to improving myself that I have no time to criticize others.

To be too large for worry, too noble for anger, too strong for fear, and too happy to permit the presence of trouble.

To think well of myself and to proclaim this fact to the world, not in loud words, but in great deeds.

To live in the faith that the whole world is on my side, so long as I am true to the best that is in me.

Christian D. Larson (1874–1954)

The Optimist's Creed

There is no outside force that can affect your life unless you give that force power with your thoughts. The greatest power is within you.

Use the power within, and realize that for your life there is nothing mightier in this world.

*H*ow do you get your attention off the bills when you are trying to attract money? You pretend, you make believe, and you create games with those bills to trick your mind into thinking good thoughts. Get your mind so busy with make-believe games of what you want that there is no room for it to send you thoughts of lack.

You are a creative being, so find the best creative way for you to turn your bills and bank statements into a make-believe game of abundance.

$\mathcal{E}$very day, or at the very least once or twice a week, take a few minutes and focus on seeing yourself in joy. Feel yourself in joy. Imagine only joy ahead in your life and see yourself basking in it. As you do this the Universe will move all people, circumstances, and events to bring you that joy. You can't be in joy if you have money worries, or health worries, or relationship problems with friends or family. So deposit some joy in the bank of the Universe as often as you can. There isn't an investment that is more worthwhile.

May the joy be with you.

*O*ur highest power is love, and it is one thing each of us has an unlimited amount of. How much love do you give to others in one day? Each day we have an opportunity to set out with this great, unlimited power in our possession, and pour it over every person and circumstance.

Love is appreciating, complimenting, feeling gratitude, and speaking good words to others.

We have so much love to give, and the more that we give, the more we receive.

$\mathcal{T}$he Universe is all good; however, in difficult situations we are often not able to see the bigger picture. Even situations we call "bad" actually have good underneath them. Look at any situation with new eyes and look for the good. If you look for it, you will most assuredly begin to find it, and then you will have burst the illusion of difficulty and allowed all the good to come forth.

*I*f you find yourself in a negative situation with someone in your life, take a few minutes each day to feel love within your heart for that person, and then send it out into the Universe. Just doing this one thing helps to remove any resentment, anger, or negativity toward that person.

Remember that feeling resentment, anger, or any negative emotion attracts it back to you. Feeling love attracts love back to you. What you are feeling for another, you are bringing to you.

"It's not what happens to you, but how you react to it that matters."

Epictetus (c. AD 55–c. 135)

*N*othing whatsoever is difficult for the Universe to create through you. You can create anything you want, and all you have to do is live in harmony with the law of attraction. You provide the mold of what you want, and then the Universe fills that mold.

Your job is easy – create the mold with your mind!

$\mathcal{P}$lato said, "Know thyself," and never were more important words spoken. You must know yourself; what you are doing, what you are saying, what you are feeling, and what you are thinking, so you can bring yourself into harmony with the law.

Know yourself.

*I*f you are complaining about things in your life, you are on the complaining frequency, and you are not in a position to attract what you want.

Get on to the frequency of good with your thoughts and words. Firstly you will feel good, and secondly you will be on the frequency of receiving more good.

$\mathscr{I}$f there was a particular house you wanted, or a particular relationship or job you wanted, and you didn't get it, the Universe is telling you that it was not good enough and did not match your dream. It is also telling you that it has something BETTER and more worthy of you.

Something better is coming... you're allowed to be excited!

*Y*ou have the power to transform negative change into positive, but you cannot do it by resisting the change. Resisting the change is choosing the negative path – you are focusing on the negative, which brings with it even more negativity, pain, and misery.

To transform the negative into positive, first look for the good and positive things in the situation. There is good in every single situation, and as you look for the good things the law of attraction must present them to you. Additionally, command that this change will bring unlimited good and positivity, and know and believe in your heart that as you command it, it must be done. This is choosing the positive path.

$\mathcal{T}$he law of attraction is the most wonderful law. It is steadfast, and gives every single person what they are predominantly focusing on. You are no exception to the law, and it is yours to use in whatever way you want.

The law cannot fail. We just have to learn how to use it correctly.

"We are what we think. All that we are arises with our thoughts. With our thoughts, we make our world."

Buddha (c. 563–c. 483 BC)

$\mathcal{G}$ ratitude is just words, words, words unless you feel it intensely and deeply. To really harness the power of gratitude you must practice, practice, and practice until you reach the greatest depth of feeling and the highest frequency.

That is gratitude at its most powerful.

$\mathcal{T}$he things that come most quickly into your life are the things that you BELIEVE in the most. You can bring to you only what you BELIEVE, so you must BELIEVE to receive what you want.

When you are afraid of something happening, by the law you attract it, although fortunately it takes real focus and persistent fear to bring it to you. The amount of emotion you invest in *not* wanting something to happen is powerful. At the same time it is also impossible to bring what you want when you hold so much fear about the outcome you don't want.

Remove your personal investment of fear from what you don't want to happen, and now use that powerful energy and direct it to what you want.

No matter what you have been thinking or feeling, your power to create something new is NOW.

What are negative thoughts? The absence of good thoughts.

What are negative emotions? The absence of good thoughts!

There is a difference between feeling gratitude and appreciation for something, and feeling attachment to something. Appreciation and gratitude are states of pure love, while attachment contains fear – fear of losing or not having what you are attached to. When it comes to something you want in your life, appreciation and gratitude attract, and attachment pushes away. If you are feeling afraid that you will not get what you want, or losing what you have, then you have attachment.

To remove the attachment, keep shifting yourself into a state of appreciation and gratitude, until you can feel that the fear has gone.

*H*ere is a way to check whether you are on track with attracting what you want. Do you feel tense and anxious about it? Are you feeling pressure or stress about when it will arrive? Feel your body, too. Is it soft and relaxed? Or is it tense? If you do have feelings of tension, you are on the wrong track, and those feelings are keeping your desire away from you. Be totally relaxed, completely calm, and without any concern of when, where, or how it will arrive.

Every time you think of your desire, deliberately relax, relax, relax, and keep relaxing your body until you can feel that the tension has completely gone.

"Think of all the beauty still left around you and be happy."

Anne Frank (1929–1945)

Diary of a Young Girl

---

*W*hen things change in our life, often we have resistance to the change. But if you understand the structure of the Universe, life, and creation, then you will understand that life *is* change, and nothing ever stands still. Everything is energy, and energy is in continual motion and change. If energy stood still, you would be gone, and there would be no life.

Change is always happening for the good of you and for everyone. It is the evolution of life.

$\mathcal{I}$f you make time to list all the things you are grateful for, and you feel the feelings of gratitude, you will feel amazing every day. Your frequency will be high and you will move through your days in love with being alive, bringing joy wherever you go, positively affecting one person after another.

When you live a life like this, everything you want will come before you even ask.

Negative thoughts and negative emotions need your attention and focus to stay alive. They cannot survive without your attention to them. If you ignore them and refuse to give them any attention, you are taking the life out of them and they will be eliminated.

$\mathcal{M}$ost people can manifest the small things quickly. This is because they do not have any resistance around the small things, and because they don't think thoughts that contradict them. When it comes to the bigger things, however, people often emit thoughts of doubt or worry that contradict those bigger things. This is the only difference in terms of the time it takes for something to manifest.

Nothing is big or small for the Universe.

$\mathcal{T}$he process of creation is always about you getting yourself into harmony with what you want. It is never about the law of attraction. One day you think good thoughts, then the next day not such good thoughts, and then the next day good thoughts, and so on.

The permanent state of believing without a shred of doubt is something you have to learn, and you get better and better at it with practice.

"[One] of the principal reasons why so many fail to get what they want is because they do not definitely know what they want, or because they change their wants almost every day.

"Know what you want and continue to want it. You will get it if you combine desire with faith. The power of desire when combined with faith becomes invincible."

Christian D. Larson (1874–1954)

Your Forces and How to Use Them

$\mathcal{T}$here are two kinds of people:

Those who say, "I will believe it when I see it."

And those who say, "To see it, I know I must believe it."

$\mathcal{B}$e aware of the big difference between inspired action and activity. Activity comes from the brain-mind and is rooted in disbelief and lack of faith – you are taking action to "make" your desire happen. Inspired action is allowing the law to work through you and to move you.

Activity feels hard. Inspired action feels wonderful.

Who is the captain of your ship? You know that if no one is steering a ship then that ship will be battered about in the seas and crash into rocks. Think of your body as a ship and your mind as the engine, and *you* as the captain of your ship!

Take charge of your ship so that you can use the power of your engine to steer the ship to the destination you want.

*Y*ou can most certainly help others through your thoughts, and they can help you. Every good thought you send to another is a living force. However, the person you are sending the thought to has to be asking for the same thing you are sending. If the person does not want it, then they are not in harmony with your thought frequency, and it will not penetrate them.

You cannot create in another's life against their will, but if it is something they want, your thoughts are a real force that helps them.

When you exist in the beautiful state of gratitude, you become a person who only wants to give. You become so grateful that it takes over your life, and you can't find enough opportunities in a day to give. You give joy, you give love, you give money, you give appreciation, you give compliments, and you give kindness. You give the best of yourself in your job, in your relationships, and to strangers.

You will know when you have really found true gratitude, because you will become a giver. One who is truly grateful cannot be anything else.

When people first start using The Secret, they may get a little scared of thinking negative thoughts. Because of that fear, when they think a good thought, immediately the opposite thought may come into their mind. This is not unusual. However, I want you to know that this phase passes very, very quickly. And the easiest way for it to pass is to pay no attention whatsoever to the negative thoughts. Just ignore them and then think a good thought. When a negative thought comes, just shrug it off as if you don't care about it one bit, and think a good thought to replace it.

$\mathcal{I}$f you want to attract money, you may find that you have more power by imagining having the things you want the money for. If there is a lack of money in your life, then your feelings and beliefs about money are most likely not very good, and thinking instead about having the things money will buy may feel much better. You have to learn to decipher your feelings and choose the thoughts that feel better to you.

The thoughts that feel better are where your power is.

"If you are distressed by anything external, the pain is not due to the thing itself, but to your estimate of it; and this you have the power to revoke at any moment."

Marcus Aurelius (121–180)

*P*ure gratitude is a state of giving. When you are in a state of heartfelt gratitude you are radiating a powerful electromagnetic field around you. The radiations from you are so pure and powerful that they touch all those you come into contact with. The effect on others who receive what you are radiating would be impossible to trace – the ripple effect from one person to another never ends.

*G*iving opens up the door to receiving. You have so many opportunities to give every day.

Give kind words. Give a smile. Give appreciation and love. Give compliments. You can give courtesy to other motorists while you are driving. You can give a smile to the car parking attendant. You can give a warm greeting to the newspaper-stand person or the person who makes your coffee. You can give by allowing a stranger to go ahead of you into an elevator, and you can give by asking which floor they are going to and pressing the button for them. If someone drops something you can give a helping hand and pick it up for them. You can give warm embraces to those you love. And you can give appreciation and encouragement to everyone.

There are so many opportunities for you to give and thereby open the door to receiving.

When you reach the highest levels of gratitude, every thought you think, every word you speak, and every action you take comes out of pure goodness.

$\mathscr{Y}$ou are an electromagnetic being emitting a frequency. Only those things that are on the same frequency as the one you are emitting can come into your experience. Every single person, event, and circumstance in your day is telling you what frequency you are on.

If your day is not going well, stop and deliberately change your frequency. If your day is going swimmingly, keep doing what you are doing.

Sometimes it is better to focus on one thing at a time, so that you harness all your energy for the one thing. That said, you can list multiple things that you want and spend one day at a time focusing on each one, feeling as though you have received it. You will most likely find that the things you have the least concern about will come first, because your lack of concern allows the Universe to easily deliver.

$\mathcal{R}$esistance blocks what you want from coming to you. You create resistance in yourself by feeling anxious or worried about what you want. That tension causes the resistance and blocks delivery.

If you feel tense when you think of what you want, it is time to relax, relax, relax. Let your body relax your mind by allowing your body to be floppy and as fluid as water. Every time you feel yourself starting to tense up, relax your body until you feel floppy again.

"A man is but the product of his thoughts. What he thinks, he becomes."

Mahatma Gandhi (1869–1948)

*Y*ou can limit yourself by the story you have created about you. Here are some simple examples of how the story we have created about ourselves can limit us:

I am no good at math. I have never been able to dance. I am not a very good writer. I am very stubborn. I don't sleep well. I am very moody. I struggle with my weight. My English is not good. I am always late. I am not a very good driver. I can't see without my glasses. It is hard for me to make friends. Money seems to slip through my fingers.

The moment you become *aware* of what you are saying, you can delete these things and rewrite your story!

*H*ere is a description of who you really are:

I AM whole.

I AM perfect.

I AM strong.

I AM powerful.

I AM loving.

I AM harmonious.

I AM happy.

Got any work to do?

$\mathscr{B}$ecome increasingly aware of all the magnificent things in your life. Feel gratitude toward all the people who have given so much through their work and inventions so that you can have a much easier life. Did you take a shower this morning? Did you use electricity? How did you get to work? By car, train, bus, or did you walk in your shoes? Did you pick up coffee or listen to the radio or make a call on your cell phone or take an elevator? You use so many inventions every day of your life. Are you taking them for granted or are you being grateful for them?

We are so blessed – really we are.

$\mathcal{T}$o practice the art of visualization, begin by thinking back on your day. Choose a wonderful scene or moment from your day, and replay that scene in your mind. Picture the place, the people, the background sounds, the colors, the words that were spoken, and every detail of that scene as you replay it in your mind.

This is a very powerful way of improving your visualization skills, and at the same time you are attracting more wonderful scenes into your life.

The Supreme Power of the Universe is the supplier of all things, and the law of attraction is the distribution manager of those things. You are a central point of creation on Earth, and it is through you and your use of the law that the Universe can bring creation into our physical world.

What a beautiful system!

$\mathcal{T}$oday is the best day of your life!

"What one knows, one sees."

Johann Wolfgang Von Goethe

(1749–1832)

---

*C*ontinually monitor how you are feeling. You want to be feeling life flowing through you like a river, rather than tensely holding on to life. You can tell by the way you feel if you are relaxed and flowing, or if you are holding tension inside you.

One way of releasing any tension is to decide that you are going to give the very best of yourself to everyone. As you give the best of you, you are opening up the flow of the Universe to move through you. And it feels so good!

$\mathcal{T}$o live *equally* balanced between your heart and your mind is to live a life of bliss. When your heart and mind are balanced, your body is in complete harmony. And so is your life.

$\mathcal{T}$hink kind thoughts. Speak words of kindness. Act with kindness. Make kindness your state of being in thoughts, words, and actions. There are many degrees of kindness, and it is interesting to realize that what people call "evil" is simply the *absence* of kindness. There is no source of evil – only the absence of kindness.

There is only One Power – and it is all positive and all good.

*U*se the power of your will and *do* the things that will change your life. Practice the principles of The Secret every day. Use the power of your will and determine to LIVE these principles. Use all the laws of nature for your benefit. Use discipline to practice every day without exception.

You are the only one who can strengthen your will. The changes you see will be in exact proportion to how much you commit to *doing* them.

*W*e now know conclusively through science that energy can never be created or destroyed – it can only change form. We are made of energy, therefore we also cannot be created or destroyed – we just change form.

Many human beings have such a fear of death, but we are eternal life that simply changes its outside form.

There is not a single instance in history where hate has brought joy to human beings. Hate destroys those who hold it in their minds and bodies. If humanity released all hate, fear, and resentment, then no dictator could ever rise, and we would have peace on earth.

Peace on earth can occur only through peace within each of us.

"The positive mind is always in harmony with itself, while the negative mind is always out of harmony, and thereby loses the greater part of its power.... In the positive mind, all the actions of the mental system are working in harmony and are being fully directed toward the object in view, while in the negative mind, those same actions are scattered, restless, nervous, disturbed, moving here and there, sometimes under direction, but most of the time not. That the one should invariably succeed is therefore just as evident as that the other should invariably fail."

Christian D. Larson (1874–1954)

Your Forces and How to Use Them

There is no past or future for the law of attraction, only the present, so stop referring to your life in the past as very difficult, or full of hardship and pain, or in any other negative way.

Remember that the law operates only in the present, so when you speak of your past life negatively the law is receiving your words and sending those things back to you NOW.

The process of creation is the same for all things, whether you want to bring something to you or remove something negative from your life.

If you have a habit you wish to break, or anything negative you wish to remove from your life, you must focus on what you want. That means you visualize and imagine yourself in that negative-free state right now. Imagine yourself in as many scenes as you possibly can where the negative situation is completely absent. Imagine yourself happy and free. Eliminate any picture from your mind of you with the negative situation. Just imagine yourself in the state you want to be in, and feel that you are that, right now.

$\mathcal{E}$very single day, no matter who you meet in the day – friends, family, work colleagues, strangers – give joy to them. Give a smile or a compliment or kind words or kind actions, but give joy! Do your best to make sure that every single person you meet has a better day because they saw you. This might sound like it is not connected with you and your life, but believe me it is inseparably connected through cosmic law.

As you give joy to every person you meet, you bring joy to YOU. The more you can give joy to others, the more you will bring the joy back to you.

$\mathcal{M}$any people who diet lose the weight and then put it back on, because their focus was on losing weight. Instead, make your perfect weight your focus.

Whatever is your strongest focus is what you will attract. That is how the law works.

*F*ocus on the wonderful things about you, and when your mind starts to criticize any part of you, stamp out those thoughts. Stop them immediately and switch your mind to the good things about you. If you focus on the good things about you, you will attract an abundance of the good things.

Be kind to yourself, because you deserve it!

*E*ach one of us is the creator of our own lives, and we cannot create in someone else's life unless the other person is consciously asking for that same thing. For example, when someone wants to be well, then others around that person can use their powerful focus of pure wellness for them. The positive energy will be received by the person because they are asking for it themselves, and it will help them enormously.

"We speak learnedly of the Law of Gravitation but ignore that equally wonderful manifestation, *the law of attraction in the thought world*. We are familiar with that wonderful manifestation of Law which draws and holds together the atoms of which matter is composed – we recognize the power of the law that attracts bodies to the earth, that holds the circling worlds in their places, but we close our eyes to *the mighty law that draws to us the things we desire or fear, that makes or mars our lives*.

"When we come to see that thought is a force – a manifestation of energy – having a magnet-like power of attraction, we will begin to understand the why and wherefore of many things that have heretofore seemed dark to us."

William Walker Atkinson (1862–1932)

Thought Vibration

Know yourself! Watch how you manifest the small things in life and think about how you felt inside with those things. Think about how easily they came. You will find that you thought of a small thing once and never thought about it again, and then it manifested.

What really happened was that you didn't think any thoughts or speak any words which contradicted what you wanted, so the law of attraction was able to do its work.

$\mathcal{T}$o understand the power and the magic of gratitude, you have to experience it for yourself. So why not begin by deciding to find one hundred things a day to be grateful for?

If you practice gratitude every day it won't take long before gratitude is your natural state of being, and when that happens you will have unlocked one of the greatest secrets to life.

What is the most powerful thing you can add to the process of creating what you want? Ask for others as you ask for yourself. An easy way to do this is to ask for ALL, which of course includes you. Ask for a good life for all, peace for all, abundance for all, health for all, love for all, and happiness for all.

When you ask for others, it comes back to you, so the law has it ALL covered.

$\mathcal{T}$he law of attraction cannot change anything in your life that you hate, because hate prevents the change from coming. Since the law is giving us exactly what we are putting out, when you hate something the law must continue to give you more of what you hate. You will not be able to move away from it. Love is the only way.

If you focus completely on the things you love, then you are on your way to a beautiful life.

$\mathscr{C}$riticism can be very subtle in the way it creeps into our thoughts. Here are some examples of criticism to help you become aware of its subtlety, so you can eliminate it from your thoughts:

The weather is awful today.

The traffic is terrible.

The service is really bad.

Oh no, look at the line.

He/she is always late.

How long do we have to wait for our order?

That motorist is a lunatic.

It's so hot in here.

I've been on hold for so long!

These are subtle things, but the law of attraction is listening to them all. You have the ability to appreciate something in every single circumstance. There is always something to be grateful for.

$\mathcal{T}$he process for manifesting what you want is the same, no matter what it is. The process is outlined so thoroughly in *The Secret* film and the book, and so if you are not clear then you should watch the film over and over again, or read the book over and over again, until it seeps into your mind. Then you will take the principles of The Secret into your consciousness and life, and you will know how to do anything.

"First keep the peace within yourself, then you can also bring peace to others."

Thomas à Kempis (1380–1471)

The Imitation of Christ

*I*magine your good feelings as rainwater, and your body as the catchment area for the rainwater.

As you make sure you feel as many good feelings as possible, you are keeping the catchment area full and overflowing. But if you forget to deliberately put the good feelings in, the water level will drop very low to the bottom where the silt and mud lie. Negative feelings are just an indication to you that your catchment area has dropped down to the silt and mud, and that you need to fill yourself up again with good feelings until you are overflowing. Keep yourself overflowing by deliberately filling yourself with good feelings every day.

$\mathcal{E}$very positive step that you take is transforming your being. With the consistent use of your will and steady determined practice of what you have learned, you will be amazed at how fast transformation takes place. Transformation of your being brings a peace and a joy that is indescribable. You have to experience it to know it, but once you do, you will never go back.

$\mathcal{Y}$ou cannot ever say the law of attraction is not working, because it is working all the time. If you don't have what you want, you are seeing the effect of your use of the law. If you don't have what you want, then you are creating *not having* what you want. You are still creating and the law is still responding to you.

If you understand this, then you can redirect your incredible power to attract what you want.

*F*loat through life and try not to resist challenges when they come. Resisting them holds them to you. Focus your mind on what you want, and then float above the challenging or negative things. Imagine you are way up in the sky and looking down on the little dot of negativity. When you do this you are detaching yourself from the negativity and seeing it for what it really is.

This one little process will keep you from drowning in a negative situation.

Begin your day by feeling grateful. Be grateful for the bed you just slept in, the roof over your head, the carpet or floor under your feet, the running water, the soap, your shower, your toothbrush, your clothes, your shoes, the refrigerator that keeps your food cold, the car that you drive, your job, your friends. Be grateful for the stores that make it so easy to buy the things you need, the restaurants, the utilities, services, and electrical appliances that make your life effortless. Be grateful for the magazines and the books that you read. Be grateful for the chair that you sit on, and the pavement that you walk on. Be grateful for the weather, the sun, the sky, the birds, the trees, the grass, the rain, and the flowers.

Thank you, thank you, thank you!

$\mathcal{Y}$ou cannot miss an opportunity, because the Universe will keep presenting them to you. If you think you have missed an opportunity you will not feel good, and you definitely won't be on the frequency to receive the right opportunity. Have faith. The Universe has unlimited opportunities to present to you, and unlimited ways to get your attention.

You will seize on the right opportunity.

"Everybody can be great... because anybody can serve. You don't have to have a college degree to serve. You don't have to make your subject and verb agree to serve. You only need a heart full of grace. A soul generated by love."

Dr. Martin Luther King Jr.

(1929–1968)

To receive something good you must get yourself onto the goodness frequency. To glue yourself to that goodness frequency, think good thoughts, speak good words, and take good actions.

*W*ithin you are the exact answers that you need to every single question, and so it is important that you discover answers for yourself. You must trust in yourself and all that you are. *The Secret* book and film help you to understand the power that is within you, and help you to become aware of that power so that you can use it.

Ask the question, and then remain intensely aware, because the answer will come to you any second.

*R*emember the three wise monkeys?

See no evil.

Hear no evil.

Speak no evil.

That means: See no negativity, hear no negativity, speak no negativity.

Those three monkeys were definitely wise!

*T*hank you! Thank you! Thank you! These two words, when fused with intense feeling, can improve your life more than you can imagine. But you must saturate the words with the feeling of gratitude in your heart.

You know what you feel when someone says "Thank you" without any feeling. You feel nothing. And you know what it feels like when someone says "Thank you" with all of their heart. The words are the same in both cases, but when the feeling of gratitude is added you can feel the effect of that energy reach you immediately.

When you put feeling into the words "Thank you," you give the words wings.

$\mathcal{I}$f you are looking for love, the best chance you have of finding absolute happiness with the perfect person (whoever that may be) is if you surrender to the Universe. Allow the Universe to bring the love of your life to you, and to move you to them. This means you have to get out of the way and become receptive to the possibilities that the Universe presents to you.

From our smaller perspective we cannot see everything, but from its total perspective the Universe knows the perfect matches.

"Kindness in words creates confidence. Kindness in thinking creates profoundness. Kindness in giving creates love."

Lao-Tzu (c. 4th century BC)

$\mathcal{S}$tress, worry, and anxiety simply come from projecting your thoughts into the future and imagining something bad. This is focusing on what you don't want! If you find that your mind is projecting into the future in a negative way, focus intensely on NOW. Keep bringing yourself back to the present.

Use all of your will, and focus your mind in this very moment, because in this moment of now there is utter peace.

$\mathscr{I}$s this a thought that you hold?

"I have no money to give, but when I have money then I will give." If it is, you will never have money. The fastest way to attract anything is to give it to another, so if it is money you want to attract, then give it. You can give $10 or $5 or $1. It doesn't matter what the amount is, just give it. It doesn't matter how much and it doesn't matter where you give it, just give!

$\mathcal{T}$he more you practice gratitude the more deeply you will feel it in your heart, and the depth of the feeling is the key. The more deeply and sincerely you feel it, the more happiness you will bring to yourself in every single area.

Watch what happens in your life when you practice gratitude at every opportunity, every single day.

Whenever you ask for something for yourself, try also asking for the world.

Good things for you – good things for the world. Prosperity for you – prosperity for the world. Health for you – health for the world. Joy for you – joy for the world. Love and harmony for you – love and harmony for everyone in the world.

It's a small thing that has incredible results.

So often when things change in our lives, we have such a resistance to the change.

This is because when people see a big change appearing they are often fearful that it is something bad. But it is important to remember that when something big changes in our lives, it means something better is coming. There cannot be a vacuum in the Universe, and so as something moves out, something must come in and replace it. When change comes, relax, have total faith, and know that the change is ALL GOOD.

Something more magnificent is coming to you!

*I*f you want to attract a better job or anything better than what you currently have, it is important to understand how the law of attraction works.

You know that to bring in something better you must imagine what that better thing looks like in your mind, and then live in that picture as though it is here now. But you should also know that if you complain about your current job, for example, and continue to focus on all the negative things, you will never bring the better job to you. You must look for the things to be grateful for in your current job. Each thing you find to be grateful for is helping to bring that better job to you. That is really working the law!

*O*bserve a person's car, and you will learn something about its owner. The cars that are sparkling clean are evidence that their owners appreciate them. The cars that are very dirty and messy are not being appreciated. One person is attracting even better cars. The other is attracting lesser cars.

Appreciation *for the things you have* is using the law of attraction intelligently.

"Resolve to remain as strong, as determined, and as highly enthused during the darkest night of adversity as you are during the sunniest day of prosperity. Do not feel disappointed when things seem disappointing. Keep the eye single upon the same brilliant future regardless of circumstances, conditions, or events. Do not lose heart when things go wrong. Continue undisturbed in your original resolve to make all things go right...

"The man who never weakens when things are against him will grow stronger and stronger until all things will delight to be for him. He will finally have all the strength he may desire or need. Be always strong and you will always be stronger."

Christian D. Larson (1874–1954)

Your Forces and How to Use Them

$\mathcal{T}$he law of attraction is a giant photocopying machine; it photocopies what we contain in our mind and sends it back to us as the circumstances and events of our lives. This is a great thing, because we are getting very clear feedback on how we are doing in our life. For example, if you are not seeing enough money in your life, you know you must create abundance in your mind and imagination so the law can photocopy that and send it back to you.

Whether your thoughts are about something real or something that is not real, whether your thoughts are about the way your life is now or about the way you want your life to be, the law of attraction is responding to those thoughts. In other words, the law of attraction does not know whether you are imagining something or whether it is real.

Now do you understand the power of your imagination?

$\mathcal{H}$ere are four fundamental things to do to manifest money using the law of attraction.

1. Think more thoughts of abundance in a day than of lack of money.
2. Be happy now, without the money.
3. Be truly grateful for everything you have now.
4. Give the best of yourself to others.

Four easy steps. You can do them if you want it enough.

$\mathcal{T}$he law of attraction has never failed anyone, and so it will not fail you. The law does not fail. When things are not appearing as wanted, it is always because the person is not using the law correctly.

The law is infallible, and so when you work in perfect harmony with the law, you *will* experience the results!

$\mathcal{S}$ometimes, when we don't have the courage to change, everything changes around us to direct us to a new path.

You cannot stop yourself from growing – evolution requires it.

$\mathcal{T}$here is nothing you cannot do, and if you approach all things in life in the right order, you will do everything you want. Live your dream on the inside first, completely and totally, and then it will manifest in your life. When you have tuned yourself on the inside so completely, you will magnetize everything you need for your dream to become a reality.

This is the law. All creation in your life begins inside of you.

"Strive to be first: first to nod, first to smile, first to compliment, and first to forgive."

Anonymous

There is great power in your words, because they are thoughts that you have given additional energy to. Be aware of what you are saying. Watch your words. It is a spectacular moment when you catch your unwanted words midstream, because it means you are becoming more conscious and aware. Yes!

The infinite Universe is like our Sun. The very nature of the Sun is to give light and life. The Sun could not exist or be a sun unless it was giving light and life. Can you imagine the Sun waking up one morning as it rises and thinking, "I am sick of giving light and life!" The moment the Sun stopped giving life, it could not exist. The infinite Universe is the same as the Sun. The very essence and nature of the infinite Universe is giving, and it could not exist otherwise.

When we are in harmony with the Laws of the Universe, we experience the joy of its continuous giving.

*I*t is important to remember that you are vibrating a frequency every second. To change the outside circumstances and shift your life to a higher level, you must change the frequency on the inside of you. Thoughts of goodness, words of goodness, and deeds of goodness lift your frequency higher.

The higher your frequency, the more good you bring to you.

When you are out of harmony with the law, you experience lack in your life, but that is just the experience you are creating. The Universe is continually giving, and so you must learn how to tune yourself with the harmony of the Universe. And the perfect melody is this: good thoughts, good words, and good actions.

The Universe is completely and utterly in love with you. No matter how many mistakes you make, no matter where you are in your life, no matter what *you* think of you, the Universe loves you for all eternity.

What is it you really want? What is the outcome you want? Your job is to hold to the outcome of what you want, and to feel the outcome as though it is here now. That is your job. The HOW it will come about is the Universe's work. So many people trip up on this and try and work out the how.

Here is a simple example. A person wants to go to an expensive college, and so they try to work out how they will get the money for college. But the *outcome* is to be at the college. The person must focus on being at that college – that is their work.

Focus on the outcome and allow the Universe to use its infinite ways to make it happen.

"Like a stone thrown into the water, thought produces ripples and waves which spread out over the great ocean of thought. There is this difference, however: the waves on the water move only on a level plane in all directions, whereas thought-waves move in all directions from a common center, just as do the rays from the sun."

William Walker Atkinson (1862–1932)
Thought Vibration

*Y*ou can be an inspiration for someone who is experiencing difficulties by not lowering yourself to their sadness, but by lifting them up through the light of your joy.

You will always know if you are being the light of inspiration by how you feel. If you can maintain your good feelings, the light of your joy is shining and bright. The moment you begin to feel heavy or not good, you will know that the negativity of the problem is affecting you, and you really must step away and restore yourself to feeling good.

You have nothing to give anyone unless the joy within you is radiating outward.

Whatever the financial situation you are currently in, it is one that you have brought into reality through your thoughts. If it is not what you want, then you have created it unconsciously, but still you created it. When you can see this you will understand how powerful you are at creating. And now all you have to do is create what you want, consciously!

When you close your eyes and you visualize having money and imagine doing all the things you want with that money, you are creating a new reality. Your subconscious mind and the law of attraction do not know whether you are imagining something or whether it is real. And so when you imagine, the law of attraction receives those thoughts and images as though you were actually living them, and it must return those visions to you.

When you are in the place where what you are imagining feels real, you will know that it has penetrated your subconscious mind, and the law of attraction must deliver it.

When you go to pay your bills, use your imagination, and make up any game you like. Imagine your bills are checks, or imagine that you are giving the money as a gift when you pay them. Add zeros to your bank statement, or put the Bank of the Universe check from The Secret website on your bathroom mirror, on your fridge, at the bottom of your television screen, on your oven, on the visor in your car, on your desk, or on your computer.

Play, pretend, and make up games that will infiltrate your subconscious with the feeling of abundance.

$\mathcal{T}$he fastest way to receive is to give, because giving starts the reciprocal action of receiving. We all receive according to how much we give. Give the best of you everywhere you go. Give a smile. Give thanks. Give kindness. Give love.

Your giving should be a giving without expectation of return – a giving for the sheer joy of it.

$\mathcal{E}$very religion on the planet has told us to have FAITH.
Faith is when you cannot see how, but you absolutely know
that the moment you have the dream it is given to you,
and all you have to do is relax and allow the Universe to
magnetize you to your dream and your dream to you.

"All that we are is the result of what we have thought.... If a man speaks or acts with an evil thought, pain follows him.... If a man speaks or acts with a pure thought, happiness follows him, like a shadow that never leaves him."

Buddha (c. 563–c. 483 BC)

The Twin Verses

$\mathscr{B}$ecause everything already exists in the spiritual world, what you want also exists, and in fact it has always existed because there is no time in the spiritual world. That can be a difficult idea for our limited physical minds to understand. But the important point is that if what you want already exists, then you will understand that the moment you ask it is given to you. And all you have to do to bring what you want from the spiritual to the material world is to emit the exact same vibration as what you want. You do not have to create what you want, as it already exists.

BE the vibration of what you want, and you will bring it into the material world through you.

When you criticize or blame anything or anyone, notice how you are feeling. Those bad feelings are telling you clearly that you are attracting negativity. Take notice of the infallible guidance that the Universe is transmitting to you through your feelings.

Feeling anything less than good is simply not worth it.

$\mathcal{H}$ere is a checklist to make sure you have your receiving channels open:

Do you receive compliments well? Do you receive unexpected gifts easily? Do you accept help when it is offered? Do you accept your meal being paid for by a friend?

These are little things, but they will help you know if you are open to receiving. Remember, the Universe is moving through everyone and every circumstance to give to you.

*Y*our thoughts and feelings are *cause* and what manifests is *effect*, so if you internalize what you are wanting you are completing all you have to do. As it is within, so it is without. As it is on the inside of you, so it is on the outside of you.

Remember, inside you is the *cause* and the outside world is the *effect*.

$\mathcal{I}$f an action in your life feels like it contradicts what you want, then use your imagination while you are doing the action. You can use your actions every day to *help* create what you want. For example, when you are driving your old car you can imagine that you are really driving the new car that you want. When you reach for your wallet you can imagine it bursting with notes. You can change any action into a game of make-believe that is in line with what you want.

Remember that the law of attraction does not know if something is real or imagined.

When I was creating *The Secret* film, I was learning the law at the same time, and for a while I made the mistake of looking for help in the outside world. I was creating a film that cost millions of dollars, and when I began I was in a lot of debt. No matter where I went or looked for help, it did not appear. One door after another slammed in my face. I was looking in the wrong place for help, because all of the power of the Universe was within me.

Once I shifted myself and connected to the power within me, and focused only on that, I allowed the Universe to find the perfect way. I did my job and held to the outcome with my heart, mind, and body, and the way lit up.

"You may freely choose what you think but the result of your thought is governed by an immutable law."

Charles Haanel (1866–1949)

The Master Key System

When you find your purpose, it is like your heart has been set alight with passion. You know it absolutely, without any doubt.

$\mathcal{T}$here is no limit to how high you can increase your frequency, because there is no limit to the good thoughts you can think, or the good words you can speak, or the acts of kindness that you can perform. Besides transforming your own life through lifting your frequency, you lift others' lives too. The positive frequency of your energy emanates out like the ripple from a stone thrown into water, touching our planet and every living thing on it.

As you rise higher, you take the world with you.

No person or power in the outside world can compare to the power you have within you. Seek the power within, as it knows the perfect way for you.

$\mathcal{Y}$ou cannot bring what you want to you if you are feeling stress. Stress or any tension at all is something you have to remove from your system.

You must let the stress go – it is the only way you can bring what you want. The emotion of stress is saying strongly that you do NOT have what you want. Stress or tension is the absence of faith, and so to remove it all you have to do is increase your faith!

*F*aith is trusting in the good.

Fear is putting your trust in the bad.

Whatever you want to bring into your life, you must GIVE it. Do you want love? Then give it. Do you want appreciation? Then give it. Do you want understanding? Then give it. Do you want joy and happiness? Then give it to others.

You have the ability to give so much love, appreciation, understanding, and happiness to so many people every single day!

"When you have made up your mind what you want to do, say to yourself a thousand times a day that you will do it. The best way will soon open. You will have the opportunity you desire."

Christian D. Larson (1874–1954)

Your Forces and How to Use Them

*N*ever let a day pass without looking for the good, feeling the good within you, praising, appreciating, blessing, and being grateful.

Make it your life commitment, and you will stand in utter awe of what happens in your life.

When a big change occurs in your life it forces you to change direction. Sometimes the new path may not be easy, but you can be absolutely certain that there is magnificence for you on the new path. You can be absolutely certain that the new path contains things that you could not have experienced otherwise.

When we look back at a negative event that occurred in the past, we often see how in fact it transformed our life. We see how that event directed us toward a life that we would not change for anything.

$\mathcal{T}$he ancient Babylonians practiced a vital law that was the cause of their immense prosperity. They used the tithing law, which involves giving one-tenth of all money or riches that you receive. The tithing law says that you must give to receive, and the Babylonians knew that the practice of this law opened up the flow of abundance.

If you are thinking, "I will give when I have enough money," then the tithing law says you will never have enough money, because you have to give first. Many of the wealthiest people on the planet tithed their way to wealth, and they have never stopped tithing!

When you look at yourself and feel dissatisfaction about any part of you, you will continue to attract feelings of dissatisfaction, because the law mirrors back to you exactly what you are holding inside.

Be in awe and wonder at the magnificence of you!

*N*o matter what the odds, we can make this lifetime the best it can be. Think of the story about Morris Goodman in the film of *The Secret*. Morris lay in hospital completely paralyzed, only able to blink his eyes. But he knew he could still use his mind to visualize, and, against all odds, Morris walked.

Visualize your life as magnificent. Visualize yourself in complete joy, and hold to that vision no matter what!

*Y*ou are a magnet. You bring to you whatever you are feeling on the inside, so be the magnet of joy, and continuously work at this with all of your might. Joy is a feeling inside you, and you can cause yourself to feel that no matter what is happening in the outside world.

Know that to live in accordance with the law you must be in joy so that a life filled with joy can come to you.

"Most folks are about as happy as they make up their minds to be."

Abraham Lincoln (1809–1865)

People go through their whole lives chasing everything in the material world, and they fail to discover the greatest treasure of all, which is within them. Shut your eyes to the outside world. Direct your thoughts and words to the inside of you. The master within you is the key to all the treasures in the world.

$\mathcal{Y}$ou have the master within you, and you are being guided in every single moment of your life. Think for yourself, and choose for yourself.

*Y*our body is exactly like a movie projector, and the film running through the projector is all of your thoughts and feelings. Everything you see on the screen of your life is what has been projected from within you, and is what *you* have put into the film.

By choosing higher thoughts and feelings you can change what you see on the screen at any time. You have complete control of what goes into your film!

*H*ow is the movie of your life going? Do you need to make any script changes on money, health, or relationships? Is there any editing that you want to do? Today is the day to make any changes to your movie that you want, because today's changes will be screening tomorrow.

You are creating the movie of your life and it is in your hands – every single day.

*A*lthough there is much to learn and much to study, the Truth of Life is in everything in the world around you, if you have the eyes to see. It is only our ignorance and fixed beliefs that blind us to the Truth.

Continue to ask questions within yourself, continue to learn, continue to let go of fixed beliefs, and the Truth will unfold within you.

"When you are inspired by some great purpose, some extraordinary project, all your thoughts break their bonds; your mind transcends limitations, your consciousness expands in every direction, and you find yourself in a new, great and wonderful world. Dormant forces, faculties and talents become alive, and you discover yourself to be a greater person by far than you ever dreamed yourself to be."

Patanjali Yoga (c. 200 BC)
Sutras

You must speak as though you have what you want now. This is very important. The law responds exactly to your thoughts and words, and so if you see something as being in the future you are actually stopping it from happening now.

You must feel it as though you have it now.

As you practice and practice the law of attraction, the vibrations of your thoughts and feelings go higher and higher. There is no limit to how high they can vibrate, and as they vibrate higher and higher your life becomes higher and higher. This is a step-by-step process however, and the only way to go higher is step by step.

So feel as good as you can each day, think as many good thoughts as you can each day, and you will get there!

$\mathcal{T}$he way to have complete control of the law is to have complete control of yourself. Control your thoughts and emotions, and you will become the master of the law of attraction because you have become the master of yourself.

No human being would ever deliberately bring anything to them that they did not want, but unfortunately throughout the history of humanity many human beings have suffered pain, sorrow, and loss because they were not aware of the one law that affects their lives more than any other.

The course of history has now changed, because you have the knowledge of the law of attraction and you can create the life you deserve. You are changing history!

*Y*our job is you and only you. When you are working in harmony with the law, no one can come between you and the Universe. However if you think another person can get in the way of what you want, then you have done a flip to the negative. Focus on creating what you want.

You are the center of divine operation in your life, and your partner is the Universe. No one can get in the way of your creation.

When you are undecided on which way to turn or what path to follow, remember there is one who knows and will guide you through every decision and turn in your life. All you have to do is ask, believe you will receive the guidance you want, and then stay alert to receive your answer. The Supreme Power of the Universe is with you every step you take, and all you have to do is rely upon its power and ask.

*I*t is when you no longer feel the need for money that money will come. The feeling of needing money comes from the thought that you don't have enough, and so you continue to create not having enough money.

You are always creating, and when it comes to money, you are either creating the lack of it or the abundance of it.

"Our destiny is not mapped out for us by some exterior power; we map it out for ourselves. What we think and do in the present determines what shall happen to us in the future.

"There is nothing in your life that you cannot modify, change, or improve when you learn to regulate your thought."

Christian D. Larson (1874–1954)

Your Forces and How to Use Them

$\mathcal{T}$he tighter you try and hold on to something that you are afraid of losing, the more you are pushing it away. Those thoughts are filled with fear, and if you continue to persist, what you fear the most will come upon you.

Fear nothing – just think about what you want. It feels so much better!

$\mathcal{T}$he truth will set you free. All the pain and suffering in the world has come from people not knowing the immutable cosmic laws of the Universe. The principles within The Secret were given to each person to prove the cosmic law for themselves. Prove it to yourself, and the truth will set you free.

*B*eliefs are created by thinking thoughts over and over and over – until they become beliefs. Beliefs are a constant frequency that you are transmitting, and our beliefs are the strongest things that create our life through the law of attraction. The law of attraction responds to what you *believe*!

That is why when you want to create something you must ask and *believe*, and then you will receive.

*Y*our true nature is love, and the proof is that you have an *unlimited* supply of it within you. No human being has a lesser amount, nor does anyone have limits on the amount of love they can bring forth from within them.

The almighty power of love ignites the law of attraction – it is the strongest magnetic force in the Universe.

$\mathcal{I}$f a person is focused on illness then they are inadvertently attracting more illness to them. On the other hand, if a person focuses more on health than illness, then the law of attraction must obey and produce health. The principles of the law of attraction are a powerful tool to summon the healing power within us, and can be used as an aid in total harmony with all of the wonderful medical procedures that are available today.

Remember that if there were no healing power within us, nothing could be healed.

*I*f you ask for something but really deep down don't believe that it can be manifested immediately because it is so big, then you are the one who is bringing time into your creation. You are creating the time it will take, based on your perception of the size of the thing you have asked for. But there is no size or time in the Universe. Everything exists *now* in the mind of the Universe!

"A strong thought, or a thought long continued, will make us the center of attraction for the corresponding thought-waves of others. Like attracts like in the thought world – as ye sow so shall ye reap...

"The man or woman who is filled with Love sees Love on all sides and attracts the Love of others. The man with Hate in his heart gets all the Hate he can stand. The man who thinks Fight generally runs up against all the Fight he wants before he gets through. And so it goes, each gets what he calls for over the wireless telegraphy of the Mind."

William Walker Atkinson (1862–1932)

Thought Vibration

You are diligent in keeping your car full of fuel. Are you as diligent in keeping yourself full with good thoughts and good feelings?

You can only go in the direction you want in your life when you have the right fuel, and enough of it.

*Y*ou are receiving thousands of messages from the Universe every single day. Learn to become aware of this communication from the Universe, who is speaking to you and guiding you in every moment. There are no accidents and no coincidences. Every sign you notice, every word you hear spoken, every color, every scent, every sound, every event and situation is the Universe speaking to you, and you are the only one who knows their relevance to you, and what the communication is saying.

Use your eyes to see! Use your ears to listen! Use all of your senses, because you are receiving communication through them all!

*R*emember to remember means remember to be aware. Remember to be aware in *this* moment right now. Being aware is seeing everything around you, hearing everything around you, feeling everything around you, and being completely focused on what you are doing right now.

Most people bring what they do not want because they are not aware that they are listening to the thoughts in their heads about the past and the future. They are not even aware that they are being hypnotized by those thoughts, and are therefore living their life unconsciously.

When you remember to be aware, you are aware immediately. You just have to remember to remember!

$\mathcal{T}$o desire something is in proper accordance with the law. You attract what you desire. To need something is misuse of the law. You cannot attract what you *need* if you feel you need it urgently or desperately, because that emotion contains fear. That kind of "needing" keeps things away.

Desire everything. Need nothing.

To create:

Step 1 – *Ask*. That means you get very, very clear about what you want by thinking it through completely. Remember that the moment you ask for what you want, it already exists in the spiritual world. Asking is the active step of creation.

Step 2 – *Believe*. That means you must know inside yourself that what you asked for is yours immediately. Your belief provides the means for your desire to transform from the spiritual into the material world. Believing is the passive step of creation.

Step 3 – *Receive*. If you believe you have already received, then you will receive. Receiving is the third step in creating, and it is the result of you bringing the active and passive together, which forms a perfect creation.

Creation is identical to a battery. Positive is active. Negative is passive. Connect the two perfectly and you have power.

*H*appiness is a state of being, and comes from the inside of you. By the law of attraction you must become on the inside what you want on the outside.

You are either choosing to be happy now, or you are making up excuses for not choosing to be happy. But there are no excuses for the law!

"We don't receive wisdom; we must discover it for ourselves after a journey that no one can take for us or spare us."

Marcel Proust (1871–1922)

In Search of Lost Time

We are not able to see everything in our future, but the supreme power of the Universe can see every possibility. In terms of relationships, you may be convinced that someone is right for you when in truth they may not be. You may be asking for a harmonious, happy, loving relationship with a particular person, but if the Universe can see that you are not able to have that happy relationship with that person, the Universe will not bring them to you.

Ask for a harmonious, happy, loving relationship, and then allow the Universe to deliver your perfect partner to you – whoever they may be.

$\mathcal{T}$he fastest way to become the master of your thoughts and emotions is through challenging situations. If your life is going along fairly smoothly, there are not the same opportunities that enable you to strengthen your power and become the master of your thoughts and emotions.

You see, even challenges are beautiful opportunities in disguise.

When you are no longer the slave to your own emotions
and thoughts – when they no longer have their way with
you without your consent – you have become the master of
your own being, and your entire life in the outside world
will be transformed. You will be the master of the law, you,
and your life.

To harness the power of well-being using visualization, imagine with every breath you take that you are breathing in pure, white, illuminating energy. Imagine your body filling with this beautiful, pure, illuminating energy, and see this energy lighting up every cell in your body until the entire inside and outside of your body is glowing and radiating like a brilliant star.

We are an exact microcosm – or mini-version – of the Universe, and when we know ourselves, we know the entire Universe.

"Know thyself," said Plato.

$\mathcal{T}$he most beautiful thing of all is that every day, in every situation, we can see how we are doing. Our world and our life are continually giving us feedback on our field of energy, and when we have begun to create a new field of energy (through good thoughts and feelings), the changes that take place around us are nothing short of spectacular.

It is worth every step and every effort, because there is nothing greater than to live in harmony with the Universe.

"Most people live, whether physically, intellectually, or morally, in a very restricted circle of their potential being. They make use of a very small portion of their possible consciousness, and of their soul's resources in general, much like a man who, out of his whole bodily organism, should get into a habit of using and moving only his little finger. Great emergencies and crises show us how much greater our vital resources are than we had supposed."

William James (1842–1910)

The reason that "now" is where all of your power exists, is because "now" is the only time you can think new thoughts and feel new feelings. We cannot think thirty seconds from now, or feel something two hours ago. We can only think NOW. We can only feel NOW. And so this moment right now is your greatest point of power.

The rest of your life awaits you!

*C*hange in a country begins with one person. Each country reflects the inner peace or turmoil of its mass population, and so as one person changes they affect the rest of the population. One person has the power within them to bring massive change to their country through immense love and peace within themselves. But you cannot bring about peace and well-being in your country unless you have conquered them in your own life. Do you see? You cannot give what you do not have.

Each person's job is to bring utter harmony into their own life, and then they will become the greatest human gift for their country and the world.

No one is destined to live a life of poverty, because each of us has the ability to change everything in this life. The law of attraction is the law of creation, and it allows each person to create the life they want. Every person has their own unique circumstances to overcome, but every single person has the opportunity to achieve anything – and change everything.

$\mathcal{T}$he future is created through our past thoughts, words, and actions. The future is the reaping of the seeds that we have sown in the past, whether those seeds are good or bad. Each sustained thought, every word we utter, and every action we take is a seed we will reap in our future.

To create a beautiful future, make as many of your thoughts as possible good ones, speak good and kind words, and make sure your actions come from goodness.

Your future depends upon it.

$\mathcal{T}$o attract whatever you want in your life, you do not work out HOW it will come about. Your work is to ask the Universe, focus on the outcome, imagine that you have it, believe that you have it, know that you have it, and give thanks that you have it now.

Do your job by vibrating your desire, and allow the Universe to do its work of bringing that desire to you.

*A*s you live in the power, the love, and the joy of your own being, you will uplift millions.

Follow your own path. Follow your own truth. Follow your own heart. Follow your own inner bliss, and allow each person to follow theirs, whatever it may be. Look for the good in everyone and everything, and let your love and joy radiate out to the world every day.

"Gratitude is not only the greatest of virtues, but the parent of all others."

Marcus Tullius Cicero (106–43 BC)

The current state of our planet is just a mirror of humanity's minds en masse. The disharmony you see on our planet is a reflection of the disharmony inside human beings. The link between our planet and humanity is a connection that cannot be broken. The world will change and our planet will change as each human being changes inside.

One human being inspires many others, and the many others inspire thousands, the thousands inspire millions, the millions inspire billions, and that is how we bring harmony to planet Earth.

It is not enough to know the principles in The Secret – you must DO them, unceasingly, every single day. You must LIVE the principles. Step by step you will become the master of your thoughts and feelings, and the master of your life.

There is nothing more important than this, because your whole future life relies on you.

*A*sk yourself if in one day you think more positive thoughts than negative. Ask yourself if in one day you speak more words of goodness, appreciation, kindness, gratitude, and love than negative words. Ask yourself if in one day you take more actions that are based in goodness, appreciation, kindness, gratitude, and love than any other actions.

In every moment of your day, there are two paths before you. Take the path of goodness, for goodness' sake.

*I*f somebody says something negative to you, do not react. You have to get yourself to a point where you can stay calm and peaceful inside no matter what negative things happen on the outside.

When you can maintain peace and joy within you despite any situation on the outside, you have become the master of everything.

$\mathcal{I}$sn't it great to know that you cannot control your world from the outside? To try to control things on the outside feels impossible because it would take so much work, and in fact it is impossible according to the law of attraction.

To change your world all you have to do is manage your thoughts and feelings on the inside of you, and then your whole world changes.

$\mathcal{R}$emember, if you are criticizing, you are not being grateful. If you are blaming, you are not being grateful. If you are complaining, you are not being grateful. If you are feeling tension, you are not being grateful. If you are rushing, you are not being grateful. If you are in a bad mood, you are not being grateful.

Gratitude can transform your life. Are you allowing minor things to get in the way of your transformation and the life you deserve?

"Whatever you are, or whatever has happened, just be glad. Be glad because you are here. You are here in a beautiful world; and all that is beautiful may be found in this world... Just be glad, and you always will be glad. You will always have better reason to be glad. You will have more and more things to make you glad. For great is the power of sunshine, especially human sunshine. It can change anything, transform anything, remake anything, and cause anything to be become as beautiful as itself. Just be glad and your fate will change; a new life will begin and a new future will dawn for you."

Christian D. Larson (1874–1954)

Just Be Glad

*G*ratitude is one of the easiest and most powerful ways to transform your life. If you become truly grateful, you will magnetize everything you need, wherever you go, and in everything you do. In fact, without gratitude, nothing can ever change. Your life will change to the degree that you use gratitude and begin to *feel* grateful. If you are just a little bit grateful, your life will change just a little bit. If you are very grateful, your life will change a lot. It's up to you.

$\mathcal{I}$t is possible to be happy and joyful most of the time. You just have to look at little children and see their natural joy. You may say that little children are free and don't have anything to worry about, but you are free too! You are free to choose worry or to choose joy, and whatever you choose will attract exactly that. Worry attracts more worry. Joy attracts more joy.

$\mathcal{T}$he most powerful way parents can help their children be positive is to be the living example of positivity and love themselves. As a parent focuses on being those things, their children will also absorb all of their positivity.

As we become more and more positive and more and more joyful, by our powerful example we uplift all of those around us.

*N*egative frequencies do not have good things on them. Get yourself onto the positive frequencies where your desires are sitting. To do that, look at every single thing in your life with NEW EYES: with grateful eyes, with positive eyes, and with eyes that only see the good.

Adjust your vision and start to see clearly. Life is spectacularly beautiful.

$\mathcal{R}$emember to keep checking on how you are feeling during the day. Check the feeling in your body and make sure your body is relaxed. If you detect any tension, then take a minute to focus on letting go and relaxing your entire body. A feeling of peace in your body and mind is your aim, because that frequency puts you on a frequency of harmony with the Universe.

*H*ave you set your intention for the day today, or are you going to let today be governed by the thoughts of yesterday? These words will help get you started.

All Good is coming to me today.

All my desires will be met today.

Magic and miracles will follow me everywhere today.

Have the best day ever!

"Men are not prisoners of fate, but only prisoners of their own minds."

Franklin D. Roosevelt (1882–1945)

When a family is creating a vision board it is important that each member of the family who is involved *wants* to be involved. It must be fun for each person. Each person in the family can then choose what they want to put on the board, without limits or restrictions. Drawings, cut-out pictures, and words are all great. Those who are the most excited will automatically focus on the board every day, and they will be the ones who manifest the things on the board into their life. The more energy given, the faster the things will manifest.

A heart on fire with excitement and passion has a huge magnetic power.

We are intelligent enough to trade in an old car when it is not serving its purpose anymore. We hand over the old car and we take possession of a newer model and continue our journey in our new car.

The greater part of you is also intelligent enough to trade in the vehicle of your body when it is not serving its purpose anymore, update to a newer, better model, and continue on your journey in the new vehicle. Human bodies and cars are vehicles – and you are the eternal driver.

Energy cannot be created or destroyed – it just changes form.

$\mathcal{T}$hink of all the good things in your life. And now realize that you brought them all into your life. Your thoughts and feelings moved the energies of the Universe to bring all those good things to you.

You are a powerful being.

$\mathcal{T}$rying to change someone is a waste of time. The very thought of changing someone is saying that they are not good enough as they are, and it is soaked with judgment and disapproval. That is not a thought of appreciation or love, and those thoughts will only bring separation between you and that person.

You must look for the good in people to have more of it appear. As you look only for the good things in a person, you will be amazed at what your new focus reveals.

$\mathcal{Y}$ou are responsible for your frequency, which is determined by your thoughts, words, feelings, and actions. As you think, speak, and act through higher thoughts of love, compassion, and goodness, your frequency goes higher and higher. Your true work in life is to keep lifting your frequency. It is the bottom line to everything, because *everything* in your life comes as a result of the frequency you are on. Everything!

"There is nothing either good or bad, but thinking makes it so."

William Shakespeare (1564–1616)

Hamlet

Work out exactly what you want. Then imagine and create games where you are pretending that you have what you want already. While you are pretending or make-believing you have what you want, be attentive to your feelings. When children make-believe, their imagination is so strong they automatically engage their feelings. Watch little children playing, and you will learn how to use the law of the Universe to your greatest advantage.

$\mathcal{R}$emember, the law of attraction doesn't know if you are make-believing or if something is real, so when you are pretending, you have to feel as though it is real. When your make-believing begins to feel real you will know that you are succeeding in bringing what you want into your reality.

$\mathcal{T}$o magnetize the things for a happier life, you have to become a happiness magnet. Happiness attracts happiness. To be a magnet of happiness requires feeling happy, thinking happy thoughts, and acting with happiness toward others. To intensely fill yourself with happiness, do everything you can to give happiness to others.

Whatever you resist will persist, which means that whatever you passionately *don't* want, you are inviting to you. Put the power of your passionate emotions into what you *do* want, and bring those things to you.

Focus is creating. Focus with emotion is powerful creating.

$\mathcal{M}$ost people don't realize how much passion they put into what they *don't* want. When you speak to a friend and you tell them all about an "awful" situation, you are putting passion into what you don't want. When you react to an event negatively, with the response that it is "terrible," you are putting passion into what you don't want.

You are a beautiful passionate being, so make sure you direct your passion wisely.

*Y*ou are in a partnership with the law of attraction, and it is through your partnership that you are creating *your* life. Every other person is in a partnership with the law of attraction as well, and they are creating *their* own lives. That means you cannot use the law against another person's free will. If you attempt it, you run a real risk of attracting your own freedom being taken from you.

$\mathcal{Y}$ou cannot use the law of attraction against someone else's free will. If you think about this deeply, and in particular in regards to love relationships, you can only come to one conclusion: thank goodness the law operates this way. If it did not, then somebody else could decide you are the love of their life, and use the law on you. They cannot do that, and neither can you.

$\mathcal{E}$very good thought you think, every good word you speak, every good emotion you feel, and every act of kindness you perform, is lifting the frequency of your being to new heights. And as you begin to raise your frequency, a new life and a new world will reveal themselves to you. You will emit positive forces of energy across planet Earth that will reach every single living thing on it.

You will lift yourself, and as you lift yourself, you lift the entire world.

We are evolving human beings, and as we grow our frequency changes. A relationship ending between two people is the *result* of the two people no longer being on the same frequency. When frequencies of people no longer match, the law of attraction automatically responds by moving them apart. Frequency change is growth, growth is life, and life is good.

*W*hat are you thinking when you open your curtains in the morning and when you close them at night? What are you thinking when you first put your shoes on and when you take them off at the end of the day? Use the power of the Universe during these four everyday actions, and say with all of your heart:

"Thank you for the most incredible day!"

*Y*ou can put positive forces into motion ahead of you wherever you go, but you have to think ahead to do it. Before you do anything, think ahead and see yourself at the completion of the action, happy, and it being completed effortlessly. Now you can move forward.

The positive forces are at your beck and call – but you have to beckon them into your life.

*M*ake your mind do what *you* want! If you are really serious about banishing negative thoughts and changing your life, then here is an easy process to help you. Every day without fail, write out one hundred things you are grateful for. When you do this you are taking control of your mind and *making it think good thoughts*. If you do this every day, you will be gaining control of your thoughts.

Make a commitment to yourself to control your thoughts. When you gain control of your mind, you will be the master of You.

$\mathcal{E}$very time you get into a car, remember to take a couple of seconds and see yourself arriving at your destination happy and well. No matter what the trip is you are taking or the type of transportation you are using, use the power of the Universe through your intention and create a beautiful, safe journey.

$\mathcal{T}$he creation process is so easy, and if you are finding it difficult it is simply because you do not believe. Remember, you have to believe it to see it! And that can be tricky if most of your life you have only believed things when you have seen them. There is some retraining for you to do with your mind. You have to believe in the unseen, and that belief is THE channel through which the unseen moves into the seen.

"Joy is not in things; it is in us."

Wilhelm Richard Wagner (1813–1883)

*C*reate vision boards with children and teach them how to play the game of visualization. Let them know that they have to make-believe that they already have what they place on the board. Children have such a wonderful imagination that pretending is second nature to them, and they will become a great inspiration for you.

"Be like little children and make-believe," are the words of truth that were spoken two thousand years ago.

No one can impact you with their negative thoughts if you are not on a negative frequency. You set your own frequency through your thoughts and feelings, and the better you feel the higher the positive frequency you are on, and the higher the thoughts you have access to. Negative thoughts of others cannot reach you there.

$\mathcal{T}$o master *believing*, all you have to do is tip the balance of your thoughts, words, and actions, from "not believing" to *believing*. The ONLY thing that can ever get in the way of manifesting what you want is having more thoughts of "not believing," speaking more words of "not believing," and taking more actions of "not believing," than you are of *believing*.

Base the majority of your thoughts, words, and actions in *believing*, and the law of attraction must obey you.

"Give every person more in use value than you take from them in cash value."

Wallace Wattles (1860–1911)

The Science of Getting Rich

$\mathcal{R}$emember this, and *never* take money from anyone without giving *more* in use value than the money you are receiving. In people's lives, this is one of the main causes of lack of money, unsuccessful job experiences, and failed businesses. Give *more* value than the money you are receiving – in your job, in your business, and in every part of your life.

*H*ave you felt gratitude for nature today?

You would not be alive today or any day if it were not for nature giving to you unceasingly. Nature is giving you an unlimited source of air so you can breathe, it is producing enough water for an entire planet's needs to keep you alive, and without the life-producing forces that the sun gives, none of us could exist.

Now that is pure giving! How could anyone believe that they are not loved?

*A*s you defend against something in your life, you are bringing the very thing you don't want to you. Defending is focusing on the problem, and defending attracts more defending. Instead, be creative and focus all your energy on the outcome you want. Creating is focusing on the solutions.

Be creative, not defensive. Focus on the solutions, not on the problems.

"I believe that the man who understands the use of thought-force can make of himself practically what he will.

"I believe that not only is one's body subject to the control of the mind, but that, also, one may change environment, 'luck,' circumstances, by positive thought taking the place of negative. I know that the 'I Can and I Will' attitude will carry one forward to success that will seem miraculous to the man on the 'I can't' plane."

William Walker Atkinson (1862–1932)

My Working Creed

*Y*our life is a learning process – you can become wiser only from learning. Sometimes you might have to attract making a painful mistake to learn something important, but after the mistake you have far greater wisdom. Wisdom cannot be bought with money – it can only be acquired through living life. With wisdom comes strength, courage, knowing, and an ever-increasing peace.

*I*f you did not have love in you, you could not be alive and exist as a human being. If you removed all the layers that are wrapped around you, peeling them off one by one, you would be left with an eternal light of consciousness that is made of pure love.

Your life journey entails peeling away the layers until you reach that core of you, which is absolute love.

No matter what you may think, you are becoming more and more every single day. No human being can go backwards. You can only go forwards and upwards.

Even when you feel things are not getting better, remind yourself – today you are so much more than you were yesterday.

*W*hen faced with a challenge that feels to you as though it is bringing negative change into your life, remember that every single thing that happens is ultimately for the good of each of us. It is not what happens, but what we do with the opportunity, and how we choose to look at it.

The Universe has to move things out to allow the better and more wonderful things to appear. Realize this change is happening because something fantastic is coming through!

" *I* am able to succeed in anything that I decide to do."

This is the absolute truth, but the point is, do *you* believe it?

*P*ure love has no conditions or boundaries. Love does not restrain itself or hold back. Love gives all the time and doesn't ask for anything in return. Love is a continuous flow without any limits. And all of this love is inside you.

"I am still determined to be cheerful and happy, in whatever situation I may be; for I have also learned from experience that the greater part of our happiness or misery depends upon our dispositions, and not upon our circumstances."

Martha Washington (1732–1802)

$\mathcal{D}$ecide that you are going to verbally express at least one thing of appreciation to *every* person you come in contact with today. The more people you see the better. Take notice of how you are feeling at the start of the day, and then take particular notice of how great you are feeling when the day has ended.

Name one day of the week as your appreciation day, and do this exact process on that day each week, without fail. And then watch what happens to your life!

$\mathcal{E}$very human being on the planet wants to be happy. Anything that anyone desires is because they think their desire will make them happy. Whether it is health, money, a loving relationship, material things, accomplishments, a job, or anything at all, the desire for happiness is the bottom line of all of them. But remember that happiness is a state inside of us, and something on the outside can only bring fleeting happiness, because material things are impermanent.

Permanent happiness comes from your choosing to be permanently happy. When you choose happiness, then you attract all the happy things as well. The happy things are the icing on the cake, but the cake is happiness.

*I*f you have a problem with a member of your family who is negative, begin by writing a list of all the things you appreciate about that person. Remember to include gratitude to them for giving you a great desire for positivity in your life, because that is a gift they are giving you. As you focus with all of your strength on appreciation, you will not only reduce your exposure to the negativity, but at the same time you will be attracting positive people into your life.

Get yourself on to the appreciation frequency, and the law of attraction can surround you only with people who are in a positive state.

*I*f you want to help someone who is having problems with their health, there is something powerful you can do. Visualize in your mind the person being strong, happy, and healthy. To do this effectively, create a scene in your mind with you and the person, and put as much detail into the scene as possible. Imagine the words you are both saying, and see the person doing things that only a happy and healthy person can do. Play that scene over and over and feel your visualization deeply as though you are really living it.

Although the person is creating their own life, this process can help them immeasurably.

*H*ave faith in the Infinite Power that is working through you. It is a pure positive power that you can direct wherever you want through the focus of your mind. However, you have to be in sync with the Infinite Power, and that means your focus has to be on the positive. When you focus on the negative, you disconnect yourself from the Infinite Power.

There is One Infinite Power and it can be used only for the positive and good.

There is a presence inside you. It is the life force that breathed your first breath when you were born. It is the life force that is breathing you now. It is a presence of unbelievable harmony, peace, and love, and it is inside you. To connect with and feel the life presence, stop, close your eyes, relax, let go of thoughts, and focus deeply on the inside of your body for a couple of minutes.

The more you do this exercise, the more the presence of pure harmony, peace, and love will arise within you.

"To promote the highest development of mind and soul, a sunny disposition is indispensable; the brighter, the happier, and the sweeter the disposition, the more easily and the more rapidly will any talent develop; and it is a literal truth that a sunny disposition is to the talents of the mind what a sunny day is to the flowers of the field."

Christian D. Larson (1874–1954)

The Great Within

What if you want to attract love and be joyously happy? But then you get caught up in the details of WHO, and you think that a particular person is the answer to your perfect relationship. The Universe can see way into the future, and it knows if a particular person will fulfil your dream or become your nightmare. When you don't receive the love of a particular person, you might think the law is not working. But it is working. Your *greatest* desire is to attract love and be joyously happy, and the Universe is saying, "Not him or not her, and please get out of the way, I am trying to deliver the perfect person to you."

Be very careful about getting caught up in the "who," "where," "when," or "how," because you could block your true desire from being delivered to you.

$\mathcal{Y}$ou are responsible for your life, and when you take responsibility for all your past mistakes, without any blame to yourself, it is proof that you have shifted your consciousness and that you are seeing the truth of your life and the law of attraction. From this new consciousness you will automatically attract the life you deserve.

*M*ost people think to ask for health only when they don't have it, but you can intend great health at any time. Use the power of your intention every single day and see yourself healthy and well.

Intend health for you and intend health for others.

*Y*ou create your future with the power of your intention. Intention is simply the conscious act of determining your future now. Health, harmony in relationships, happiness, money, creativity, and love will come to you in the future, based on your intentions now.

Intend every day and create your future life.

*W*hen you read *The Secret* book or watch the film of *The Secret*, you can take into your mind only the knowledge that is on the same frequency as you at the time. The next time you read the book or watch the film, you take in much, much more. And this process never stops. You will continue to discover something more in every reading or viewing, and the principles become clearer and clearer and clearer. That is because your consciousness is expanding *every single time*.

$\mathcal{T}$oday, be grateful. Be grateful for your favorite music, for movies that make you feel good, for your phone that connects you with people, for your computer, and for the electricity that lights up your life. Be grateful for air travel that flies you everywhere. Be grateful for the roads and traffic lights that keep the traffic in order. Be grateful to those who built our bridges. Be grateful for your loved ones, for your child, for your pet, for your eyes that enable you to read this. Be grateful for your imagination. Be grateful that you can think. Be grateful that you can speak. Be grateful that you can laugh and smile. Be grateful that you can breathe. Be grateful that you are alive! Be grateful that you are You!

Be grateful that there are two words that can change your life, and say them over and over again.

Thank you! Thank you! Thank you!

"There is no duty more obligatory than the repayment of kindness."

Marcus Tullus Cicero (106–43 BC)

$\mathcal{T}$he law is exact, the law is precise, and it never fails, so when it appears that it isn't working, you can be guaranteed it is not the law that is failing. The error can only be with the person using it. This is great news! Didn't it take practice to walk? Didn't it take practice to drive? With practice you could walk, and with practice you could drive.

Practice is all that stands between you and everything!

$\mathcal{T}$he Game of Life is about creating powerful ways of believing so that you receive. Whatever big thing you are asking for, consider having the celebration *now* as though you have received it.

$\mathcal{T}$here is no excuse not to give two minutes today to intend your tomorrow.

$\mathcal{B}$e creative and use powerful actions in line with what you want. If you want to attract the perfect partner, then make room in your closet. If you want to attract a new house, then tidy up your current house so it is ready for easy packing. If you want to take a trip, then get out your suitcases, surround yourself with pictures of the location, and put yourself in the pictures.

Think about what you would do if you had your desire, and then take creative actions that make it clear you are receiving it now.

Thank you. Thank you. Thank you. Thank you. Thank you. Thank you. Thank you.

To improve any day immediately, say and feel "Thank you" seven times in a row.

$\mathcal{T}$he law of attraction is precise, and when you do not get the results you want, it is only through your misuse of the law; instead of bringing what you want, you are creating *not* bringing what you want. But either way you are still creating.

The law is infallible and it is always responding to you.

"Everything that we see is a shadow cast by that which we do not see."

Dr. Martin Luther King Jr.

(1929–1968)

Measure of a Man

$\mathcal{T}$ake the seven days of the week and change your entire life by powerfully using the law of attraction. Begin with just one day if you want, and make that day a habit for a few weeks before adding another day. Do what works best for you, as the most important thing is that you *do it*.

Good Thoughts Monday

Every Monday is your day to intend that you are going to think only good thoughts. Think good thoughts for you and think good thoughts for others. Refuse to give your attention to anything that will not produce good thoughts. Command and determine with all of your will at the beginning of the day that, *"I have thought thousands of good thoughts today."* On average, humans think well over 50,000 thoughts a day, so you have 50,000 opportunities to think good thoughts today.

Appreciation Tuesday

Every Tuesday is your day to *appreciate, appreciate, appreciate.*
Appreciate the weather, your clothes, transport, great
inventions, your home, your food, your bed, your family,
your work colleagues, the person who serves you, your
health, your body, your eyes, your ears, and all of your
senses. Especially appreciate the past great times in your
life and the great times of the future. And finally, appreciate
that on every Appreciation Tuesday you are creating an
incredible life!

Good Deeds Wednesday

Every Wednesday is your day to fill your account at the Bank of the Universe with good deeds. Give encouragement to those around you. Give kindness. Give good words to those you see and speak to. Give a bigger tip today. Give a gift for no reason. Open doors for others. Buy coffee or lunch for someone. Give compliments. Give your smile to everyone. Give your genuine interest to those who serve you in your day. Give your undivided attention to those close to you. Give kindness to other drivers. Give your seat, and stand so that others may sit. Look for opportunities to do good deeds and the law of attraction will flood your Good Deeds Wednesday with an abundance of them.

As you give your all to Good Deeds Wednesdays, the Universe will respond, and it will become the best day of your week by far.

Thank You Thursday

Every Thursday is your day to say and feel "Thank you" in as many ways as you can. Write a list of all the people and events you want to give thanks for. Return thanks today to those who have done things for you. As you walk say "Thank you" in your mind with each step you take. As you drive, make each time you stop your cue to say "Thank you." At various times in the day, think and feel "Thank you" inside you seven times in a row. Look for every opportunity to say "Thank you" to other people, and say it with so much meaning that the person looks right at you. Thank your way through every Thursday, and make "Thank you" your predominant thought, feeling, and words of the day.

"Thank you"– two words, inconceivable potential power, and all they need is *you* to put the power into them by expressing them. Thank you!

Good Feelings Friday

Every Friday is your day to harness and magnify all the good feelings within you.

Today as you move through the day, give all of your attention to how you are feeling. Keep filling yourself up with more good feelings and more good feelings. To fill yourself to overflowing with good feelings, fill your day with what makes you feel good. Listen to your favorite song. Buy your favorite lunch. See your favorite friend. Do the things you love and that make you feel so good that you are brimming over with good feelings and cannot take the smile off your face. You will be so overflowing with good feelings you will float through the whole day.

Lighten Up Saturday

Every Saturday is your day to feel as free as a bird, to feel as free as you did when you were a child. Play! Have fun! This is the day to find your bliss and live it.

Do the things that make you feel wonderful. Do the things that make you laugh. Do the things that make you jump for joy. Dance, sing, skip, and whistle your way through the day. Celebrate your life today! As you play, laugh, smile, and have fun, you lighten up. When you have lightened up you have released negativity. The lighter you feel, the more negativity you have released. Saturdays are your days to Lighten Up!

Remember, life is a never-ending game and you will be playing the game for all of eternity.

All Good Sunday

Every Sunday take a moment to look back at the past week
and remember *all the good things*. Look ahead into the next
week and see *all the good things*.

Now you can rest because your creation is perfect and you
are satisfied that it is All Good.

$\mathcal{Y}$ou are in the perfect place on your perfect journey. You are right where you are meant to be, because you chose it. In fact, you could not be more perfect than you are now.

About Rhonda Byrne

Rhonda began her journey with *The Secret* film, viewed by millions across the planet. She followed with *The Secret* book, a global bestseller, available in 50 languages and with over 24 million copies in print worldwide.

The Secret has remained on the *New York Times* bestseller list for 198 weeks, and was named by *USA Today* as one of the top 20 bestselling books of the past 15 years.

She continued her groundbreaking work with *The Power* in 2010 and *The Magic* in 2012, also *New York Times* bestsellers.